EAT YOUR
BLUES AWAY

"Disappearing" Depression by
Changing How You Eat

Copyright © 2018 by Hunter's Moon Publishing

ISBN Paperback: 978-1-937988-42-5
ISBN Kindle: 978-1-937988-43-2

Hunter's Moon Publishing
http://HuntersMoonPublishing.com

Photo Credits:

About the Author – Rob Frado
Back Cover – Landry Major Photography

Disclaimer

I am not a medical doctor, and the views and opinions expressed in this book are not intended as a substitute for professional medical advice and counsel. They are based on my own training and experience.

You should consult with your doctor and seek the advice and counsel of your health care provider before making any changes including changes to how you eat and changes regarding any vitamins and/or supplements you may take.

Dedication

Each of the chapters in this book addresses a subject that could have an entire book written about it, and they probably have been written. I want to tell the story from the point of view of someone who has lived with depression and has come out the other side of that dark tunnel. I am victorious, and my story is not learned from a text book. My story is from the school of hard knocks, lots of Paxil and many bouts of tears.

My goal here is to introduce you to the miracle that happened to me and to have you know and believe it can also happen to you. I want to give you an overview of what is possible in the hope that it whets your appetite for the health renaissance that can be yours!

Acknowledgements

There are a few people who helped me along the path to publishing this book whom I want to acknowledge and thank.

I want to thank Janet Morano and Susan Ernst. Janet is the manager of my real estate office at Coldwell Banker Residential Brokerage, and she has given me the space to spread my wings and go down a new and different path... that of exploring the subject of health and wellness while still continuing to practice real estate. Janet gave me the venue to give my first live presentations on healthy eating for our office, and I am grateful for the opportunity. Susan is my administrator who has been my support and my friend both in real estate and personally. I am fortunate and very grateful to them and to my office for their support.

Key in the creation of this book is my friend and mentor, Connie Ragen Green; without her support, guidance and encouragement, this would not have happened. She is the person who first invited, no, strongly encouraged me to reveal my "health condition" as I referred to it with her. If not for her, I would still be in hiding about my depression. At that time, I viewed it as shameful, a disability; now I realize admitting it is a gift that is allowing me to reach out and help others.

Thank you to Steve Lundborg who picked the title of this book out of thin air on a call with me and with our friend, the late Geoff Hoff.

Most importantly, I want to thank my partner in life, Rob Frado, who has been my "why" for thirty-five years now. Thank you for believing I could do this.

"Everyone comes with baggage.
Find someone who loves you enough
to help you unpack."

~Unknown

Thank you Rob...

Be sure to pick-up Cheryl's free guide to help

end your emotional eating in 7 days!

http://EndYourEmotionalEating.com

Table of Contents

Foreword

Meeting Cheryl Major was a kismet moment for me. I was writing for a local newspaper and handled their Person-of-the-Week column. I'd find some folks in town through my own channels and my editor would find the rest.

The editor called me and asked me to interview Cheryl who was instrumental in gaining a Massachusetts State House vote to ban dog and cat devocalization practices (some call it "debarking") making this ban the first in any US state. Given my own involvement with animal rights I figured I would have some good questions for her.

We met at a local coffee shop and spent close to two hours having what was more of a conversation than an interview.

Since that time, I have grown to know Cheryl in so many ways beyond our first topic of conversation. Her approach to animal rights was just the tip of the iceberg but did set a strong foundation of her character. She was and is caring, kind, determined, smart, and approachable.

We continued to meet for tea or lunch and grew our friendship. Her support of me through difficult times was one of the anchors I clung to during a particularly stressful time in my life. As I got to know her better she continued to be the person I admire today.

We talked about many things including our struggles with mental health. I suffered from panic attacks since I was a child and she struggled with depression. When she first told me of her depression she asked me not to repeat that to anyone. She was taking medication for it and did not want that to become common knowledge. So strong was the social stigma then which has only slightly decreased today.

As she told me her life story - as friends often do - I saw a pattern of caretaking throughout her life. Parents, friends,

1

niece, husband, sheep, pets. It was a thread that wove many of her stories together and I felt we shared a lot of the same maternal instincts.

Cheryl and I hadn't met for close to a year though we kept in touch via email. We were both busy with careers and caretaking. When we did finally meet for a glorious cup of tea and an overdue hug, she told me the story of her husband's developing health issues which included waves of depression.

I could tell that Cheryl had even more concern for Rob's depression than her own. Those caretaking impulses are strong with her. She shared with me that he had been on medication for high cholesterol because of his family history but appeared to be experiencing this scary side effect. So she told me she was going to try changing their diet (which was already healthier than mine, I thought) to see if that helped.

We met up again not too long after that and she shared her surprise at how much better Rob was doing. The side effects were disappearing and he was starting to feel better. She also told me that she had stopped taking her own antidepressant medication a while ago.

The next time I saw Cheryl she seemed so free and happy. Rob was doing great, she was feeling better, and she wanted to share this great news with the world. She looked and sounded uplifted and light. This caretaker looked like she didn't have a care in the world.

It wasn't long after that Cheryl started to talk about ways to help others with what she had learned. We talked about social media and holistic practitioner classes. She was starting to build a website and blog about her experiences and looking into seminars to attend. It was clear this was a passion that she just could not keep to herself.

Cheryl started to produce and star in a weekly program for a local cable station with each week being a focus on a different topic related to healthy eating. The spots started as Cheryl speaking with powerpoint slides in between. In a short time the spots grew to include cooking lessons. She wrote columns for the local news sites and was speaking at conferences.

Always during this time Cheryl spoke about her goals as they related to helping others, never about boosting her own celebrity. Her genuine concern - her caretaking - was of those who she successfully reached.

As I witness this transition, I am often amazed at the fact that Cheryl has never once tried to change my diet or medication decision. Not once.

I admire her for respecting that everyone is in a different place and will change when they are ready. Cheryl's change was sparked by a desire to help someone else. In that way, she changed herself.

You will find that by reading Cheryl's advice and story that she makes so much sense. She takes her research seriously and then writes through her own experience. And it's all for you. Are you ready?

~ Kathy Nolan Deschenes

Preface

I know the word cure is a four letter word, and while I can't use it relative to other people, I certainly have the right to use it when discussing my own medical history.

The fact is that I "cured" my own depression by changing how I eat. I did it completely by accident, and it was an accident that totally changed my life.

I had been assured by my doctor that my depression would worsen as I got older. He was wrong.

I am writing this book because what happened to me is too important and life changing not to share with others. I would be remiss in my desire to help others if I were not to share my journey from being a person who lived with chronic depression for most of my adult life to someone who no longer lives in the shadow of depression. That is not to say that I am unaware that I tend to be sensitive to depression. My life however is no longer one of daily fighting and struggling with depression, and it is the most liberating shift you can possibly imagine.

I write this book in an effort to share my journey...that it may help others move out of the shadows of depression as I have. If you have ever struggled with depression, you will understand what is in these pages. If you have no clue what I'm talking about, I envy you...

Introduction

*"Our brains allow us to adapt and change
-- to write and rewrite who we are."*

~ Sandra Marinella

I am a recovering depressed person. Until relatively recently, I've lived most of my life struggling with some level of chronic depression. The first time I admitted this in public, I was scared to death on so many levels. Afraid of the admission; afraid of the stigma...what people might think; afraid to admit I wasn't as together as I tried to appear to be and so on.

The admission came after the recovery began, and the admission was the beginning of so much more for me. It allowed me freedom from hiding my depression. Admitting it opened new doors and opportunities to help others, something that has always been a driving force in my life and my dearest wish as my legacy.

What follows has been written in an effort to weave my personal story together with facts and information that will help you understand how I affected the miracle that has happened to me. My wish is that it may help you or someone you know with recovery from depression.

I've read books on depression written by medical professionals, and for me, I felt they were clinical...they lacked the voice of someone who truly knew depression. What I heard was the voice of someone who was schooled in the objective knowledge about the subject rather than the boots on the ground experience with it. Maybe what was missing was the pain in the writing. I don't know. I hope what I'm about to share here comes across as real as it was. You have the power to change your life and to change your mental and physical being. Many of the secrets to creating these changes are found in these pages.

The information in this book is all part of my journey, and believe me, it has been a journey! In fact, it's an ongoing journey as I continue to learn and discover more information about the connection between what you eat, what you expose yourself to in your environment and what you "feed" your brain.

In all honesty, it's also an ongoing journey in the sense that once you realize you have a tendency toward depression, you are always careful and aware. Regardless of whether you deal with depression or not, life is not always fun; often it is challenging, and it can affect our mood even on the best of days. My goal is that what follows gives others hope that they too can have natural control over challenges with depression. Life is not linear; neither is dealing with depression.

SECTION I

My Life Before – Dealing with Depression

"That's the thing about depression: A human being can survive almost anything, as long as she sees the end in sight. But depression is so insidious, and it compounds daily, that it's impossible to ever see the end."

~Elizabeth Wurtzel, Prozac Nation

Living with Depression

I look around me as I drive, and I notice the trees with their leaves turning red and gold. I see them reflected in the still water of the Waltham Reservoir in Massachusetts. I - look - around - me... I - see... I - notice. This may not seem exceptional to you, but it is to me. As someone who has spent so much time "in my head" and struggling with chronic depression, especially as fall sets in, this is truly remarkable to me!

I know writing this book will take me back to a place I don't want to be and to feelings I don't want to remember feeling anymore. I don't plan to spend a lot of time in that place though. It is my sincere hope that in reading about this journey, you may find a way out of your darkness and escape from the dark cloud that wafts in uninvited and unforewarned. If this helps you, it will be worth it. For anyone who has struggled with depression, all this may sound familiar. If you have no clue what I'm talking about, lucky you. I envy you.

What follows is the story of how I cured my own depression quite by accident. In fact, I was only trying to help someone else when it happened. An additional unexpected surprise was that I lost 20 lbs in the process...without trying to diet!

CHAPTER ONE
What It Was Like For Me

"Some memories never leave your bones. Like salt in the sea; they become part of you... and you carry them."

~Unknown

Living with depression is hard work. It can be exhausting trying to fool the world into thinking you're fine when you wake up depressed, and honestly, you don't even want to get out of bed. You're not out there living your life. The best way I can try to explain the feeling is that you are "in your head"; you're not out in the world. Your focus is small and looking inward. Sometimes it felt to me as if I were in a big deep hole in the ground, and I couldn't climb out of it...I could just look at the world from down in the hole with my eyes at ground level.

I would get dark disturbing thoughts that would usually be a sign that a bout or wave of darker depression was about to set in. It felt as if a black cloud would appear over me...just drift in. You might think you were having an "ok" day, and then these dark thoughts and that dark cloud would appear.

On a regular basis, even on "good days", I would mentally stop and check in with myself to see how I was doing that day. How I was feeling? There was never a sense of being confident in my mood or in my happiness at the times when I did feel happy. Really, I just wasn't happy; but it was more than that. It was a lack of being secure in my mood; it was not being able to trust myself.

Sometimes it would be hard to concentrate on my work because my depression would be worse. My pride in my work ethic, which had been instilled in me by my parents, made me push through my own pain and self doubt and put my clients' needs ahead of my own. Honestly, I think the ability to do that kept me going many times when I really wanted to stop and curl up in a ball.

My worst depression was often event driven; the most severe bouts were triggered by personal loss, family deaths... my younger sister, my father, and then my mother.

Most debilitating for me was the depression that set in after the death of my younger sister. We had been inseparable as kids and as young adults, although in the most recent years before her death, physical distance and having very different lives had made us less so.

I almost let her death destroy me. Part of it was abject sorrow and loss. Part of it was guilt that she was gone, and I was left behind. She had 4 small children; the eldest was only eleven when she died. It's a hard thing to comprehend why someone like that is gone and you, 3,000 miles away and unable to do much to help, are still around. Looking back, and certainly not to minimize my sense of loss, the depth and duration of my grief was in large part due to the fact that I was simply a depressive person. What should have been a "normal" grieving process morphed into years of a downward spiral of worsening depression.

At the time of my sister's death, I had been a full time Realtor for about 4 years. I was so distraught after her death that I decided to stop selling real estate for a year. One of our office administrators left around that time, and I stepped in to do that work. I couldn't cope with the general public out in the world of buying and selling real estate. I remember telling someone if I heard "the closet isn't big enough" one more time, I was going to strangle somebody. In my world of grief, people just didn't get what was important, and believe me, it wasn't the size of the closet. I just couldn't cope; I couldn't do my job anymore.

I often wondered what it was like to be happy and to have fun. I supposed it was just not in my nature or my upbringing or something like that. My family message had always been pretty consistently: work – good; fun – bad. I loved to hear people laugh with delight, and I envied them their laughter. I wondered why I was different, and that feeling of being different made me feel even worse.

"Comparison is the thief of joy."
~Theodore Roosevelt

I would change that to," "*Depression* is the thief of joy." It can be lurking out there, ready to take over, or it can be all consuming. It's so hard too that if you're not depressed, you don't have any idea what it's like; if you're not depressed, that lack of awareness is not your fault. It's hard for people who *are not* depressed to be *around* depressed people never mind live with them! They can try to relate, try to understand, but it's such a chemical thing, they just can't…and again, it's not their fault.

Sometimes people think it's all in your head; if you just change the way you think or you practice some positive affirmations, it will all change. Would that it were that simple.

It's a hard thing to describe, and I'm not sure one person's depression would be described the same as another's. I've only experienced mine thank goodness. That's more than enough for me.

For me, I think that along with the depression, I learned as a child to look for sadness rather than joy. My father had lived a very tragic early life, and I think he had an effect on me and on my outlook in that way. I now realize his struggles made him inward and very private. I think it was a coping mechanism, and while I don't think he was necessarily a depressive person, I think somehow I learned from him to look for and find sadness in the things around me rather than happiness and joy.

Depression makes you sad, and it makes you so very tired. It made me enjoy hearing other people laugh because I couldn't. Depression felt to me as though I was totally in my own head and not out in the world. Negative thoughts and feelings played in my head on a torturous never ending loop. I couldn't wait to go to sleep so it would stop, but sleep didn't last long as another symptom of depression is waking up at 3 or 4 am unable to sleep. In the morning, you don't want to get up because you're tired from not sleeping, and you just don't want to face your day. It's exhausting, sad and hopeless.

Depression can cause physical pain as well. I can't say I experienced that symptom with my depression, but I have read that quite a few people do. I got a pass on that one.

Depression affects self confidence. I have often wondered what I could have done if I hadn't had the weight and the struggle with the heaviness that came with depression. I felt alone and ashamed. Depression made me feel less than I should have been, and I didn't want anyone to know. I was afraid people would find out. I worried they might think less of me or even worse, not hire me because they would think I wouldn't do a good job. For me, depression became a disability.

My depression affected my relationships. In fact, looking back, it affected my self confidence to a large degree. When depression takes over, it colors both personal and professional successes and failures. I remember thinking I should be more confident; I had a lot going for me, but I felt like I was always observing myself from the outside. I've often wondered what I could have accomplished by now if I hadn't spent so much time and energy battling depression and trying to fool the world.

I have a friend whom I have known for over 30 years. She didn't know about my struggle with chronic depression, and when I finally "came out" as a recovering depressed person, she was upset I never told her. She was hurt I didn't trust her, but how do you trust others with what you're hiding when you don't trust yourself?

The things I missed were many. Key among them was being able to be "in the moment". I watched myself and my interactions with others with a critical eye as if I were an observer rather than a participant. I enjoyed listening to Rob laugh at things he thought were funny on TV; he could really laugh while I just couldn't. I've often said I'd rather listen to him laugh than to watch what was making him laugh. Many times, if he were watching TV upstairs while I was making dinner, I could hear him laughing at some funny videos or silly stuff. I would just listen from downstairs and wish I could do that too. Maybe It's hard for you to understand, but I got vicarious pleasure from listening to someone else really laugh.

I was always so serious. Part of it, I realize now, was my upbringing and my birth order. I was the eldest of three girls in a strict Protestant home. I had a sister who was still born who would have been several years my senior. I've often wondered how not being the eldest child would have changed my life and might have changed who I became.

Vacations? They were evaluated rather than lived. Fun was not really fun, at least not for long. If I went through a good period, there was no confidence or trust that a happy mood was genuine or could be counted upon to last. I always felt I was on the outside looking in and observing even when I was feeling better for a time.

If any of this resonates with you, then you either realize you struggle with depression or have some pretty serious questions about whether you do.

In the next chapter, I want to share a few simple questions you can ask yourself to give some direction as to whether depression may be an issue for you.

CHAPTER TWO

What are the Symptoms – A Simple Quiz for Depression

"Depression sucks... the life out of you."

~Cheryl A Major

There are many books about depression by medical people I would bet have never personally experienced depression, but who have all the schooling to "understand" it (as much as it is truly understood). They may have the best of intentions, but I can always tell if the writing comes from the heart and from experience or simply from a textbook.

Because depression truly colors your life, and can affect your emotions, your energy, sleep patterns, mental functions, etc., the first step is to ask yourself a few questions to determine if depression may be an issue for you.

Your emotions - While it's normal to have an "off day", prolonged feelings of sadness for no apparent reason are not normal. Events happen in our lives that make us feel sad, and that's appropriate. Feeling appropriately sad is very different from depression. Along with feeling sad, emotions that accompany depression may include feelings of being overwhelmed, feelings of hopelessness, loss of interest in things you used to enjoy, and in extreme cases, thoughts of suicide. It's important to ask yourself if you ever feel any of these emotions on a regular basis.

Your energy level - If you feel tired all the time or nearly all the time, you may be dealing with depression. Your gene pool may allow depression to be triggered. That is possible, but like other diseases, just because someone in your family suffers with depression does not mean you have to as well. Research is continuing to show that what we eat and are exposed to in our daily lives can turn on the genes that manifest disease. The trick here is to eat and adopt a lifestyle so you don't turn on those genes. We'll discuss this in more detail in Chapter Twelve.

Sleep - Sleeping too much or not enough may be a symptom of depression. It may seem odd, but depression can manifest as sleeping or as not being able to sleep. Either is possible as a symptom. Waking up at 3 or 4 am is a classic symptom and, as I've mentioned, one that plagued me for years!

Weight - A change in weight of more than 5% in a month, either gaining or losing, especially if you haven't been trying to gain or lose weight, may be an indication that you are dealing with depression. Depression can affect your appetite which we most often expect will be manifested as weight *gain*, but it can also lead to weight loss.

Unexplained Aches & Pains - Depression can cause real physical discomfort and may be the culprit if you are experiencing unexplained physical aches and pains. Although I never experienced aches and pains as part of my depression, many people with major depressive disorder also experience physical symptoms which can include headaches, stomach pain, back pain, etc.

Thinking & Concentrating - Difficulty thinking, concentrating, or making decisions may be associated with depression. Always being preoccupied with how awful you feel is a major issue. For me, and with the way my depression manifested, I was so busy inside my head trying to deal with my daily life that thinking about life on the outside in the real world was an ongoing challenge. It's interesting to note that, according to the World Health Organization, depression is considered to be among the leading causes of disability worldwide.

You don't have to experience every symptom listed here to be dealing with depression. I didn't check every one of them off on my list of complaints and challenges, but I was certain I was dealing with depression.

CHAPTER THREE

Is Seasonal Affective Disorder or SAD Part of Your Depression?

"Although the world is full of suffering, it is also full of the overcoming of it."

~ Helen Keller

Such an appropriate acronym: SAD. I now realize Seasonal Affective Disorder, or winter blues as it is often referred to, was part of my struggle with depression. I always seemed to feel worse, more down and depressed, as fall approached and morphed into winter. The shadows and the light changed, the days grew shorter, the flowers and plants where I live here in the Northeast froze and died. I still remember being in the house where I grew up and being aware of how the light was so different in my bedroom in those fall afternoons. It was just depressing, and it just made me feel so sad.

During the years I lived with depression, I did not have this awareness however. When you are depressed, it's often difficult to step back and look objectively at how you're feeling and then assess it based on your environment, time of year, etc. Being depressed always seemed to make everything so much harder. That feeling of being in a big hole standing on my toes with my eyes at ground level trying to see the outside world would come on strong in the fall. I would just try to make myself see the outside world, never mind trying to be present in it or in my life.

If you find fatigue, depression, hopelessness, and social withdrawal are things you struggle with at certain times of the year and it reoccurs annually, you may be struggling with Seasonal Affective Disorder.

I want to discuss Seasonal Affective Disorder again in Chapter Three, because I want to share with you the things I discovered that helped me manage my own SAD. Things I put into place to help me while I was still dealing with chronic depression. But first, I want to be sure you understand the difference between the two schools of medicine and what that means for you when you decide it's time to seek help with your depression.

SECTION II

There are Two Schools of Thought in Medicine

"The good physician treats the disease; the great physician treats the patient who has the disease."

~William Osler

Did you know there are two basic schools of thought when it comes to medicine? The definition of each and how we are handled, or treated, by the practitioners of each school when we have a health issue is important to understand.

Our typical health care system is based on allopathic medicine. Allopathic medicine is a method of medical practice which attempts to combat disease by the use of drugs and/or surgery to produce effects different from those produced by the disease being treated.

Frankly, I don't think of this as health care; I think of it as sickness care. You do whatever you want to do and eat whatever you want to eat until you get sick, and then you go to the doctor for "health care". That just doesn't make any sense to me, because this approach treats the symptoms of illness, not the root cause of the illness.

On the other hand, functional medicine is medical practice and treatments that focus on how the body and its organs are functioning. It usually involves employing the systems of holistic or alternative medicine. This is the opposite of allopathic medicine, because it searches for the cause of the illness rather than simply suppressing or masking the symptoms the patient is experiencing.

So, allopathic medicine is based on treatment or suppression of symptoms, often using prescription drugs and by specialists while functional medicine questions everything. What might be causing the symptoms that sent you to the doctor? How are your different organs working, or not working, in harmony to cause your symptoms?

CHAPTER FOUR

Allopathic medicine vs. functional medicine – what are they and how do they differ?

"The art of medicine consists in amusing the patient while nature cures the disease."

~Voltaire

If you carefully read the previous descriptions, which seems the better choice for your long term all encompassing health?

If you go to an allopathic practitioner, which I did, they will evaluate you and your mental condition to satisfy themselves as to whether you are depressed or not. If they determine you are depressed, they will then prescribe a drug to boost your production of serotonin which they maintain will alleviate your depression.

Unless you are very aware, have done your own research or are lucky enough to know people who have travelled the road on which you are travelling and have sought alternative solutions, it's important to further understand Allopathic medicine and Functional medicine. What are they, and how do they differ? Which would be a better option for you? It's good to have options, and frankly, today you need to advocate for yourself because the big medical machine does not explain your options. I took a ticket and got in line for the allopathic route. At the time, I didn't know any differently. I wasn't offered another option. The allopathic route didn't get rid of my depression. Not ever, not at all.

In the simplest of explanations, allopathic medicine is the term commonly used today by proponents of alternative medicine to describe the modern scientific system of medicine that is our current default norm of medical treatment. It promotes the use of pharmaceutical agents to suppress symptoms of diseases and conditions. In case you are unaware, depression is now considered to be a mental illness. Lovely. But later I'll share with you how I resigned from the "club" of the chronically depressed with the hope that you may follow in my footsteps, so stick with me. Good stuff is ahead!

Allopathic medicine features specialists in the various organs, such as a cardiovascular specialist, a pulmonary specialist, a neurologist, a psychiatrist and so on. Do you see an inherent problem here? Can you tell me one organ in your body that functions by itself, that is not dependent upon or does not work in conjunction with other organs? Does your heart beat without your lungs functioning? Does it beat without your brain functioning?

Here's an even more baffling question; why don't doctors ask us what we're eating when we go to them with a complaint? Doesn't it make sense that what you're feeding your body may create good or not so good results as far as your health and well being are concerned? If this hasn't occurred to you, you're not alone. In fact, it didn't occur to me until I went to see a holistic chiropractor many years ago. I don't remember what my complaint was, but I do remember the experience. This doctor did not have any bedside manner at all, but he was brilliant. He came into the room with his head down, reading the answers to the questionnaire I had filled out in the waiting area.

He didn't look up or introduce himself; he simply asked in a very monotone voice, "What are you eating?" This took me completely by surprise, and I asked him to repeat the question: "What are you eating??" I was so surprised, I'm embarrassed to say I couldn't remember what I had eaten that day. I got through the appointment, and I've never forgotten the question or how odd it seemed to me at the time. No other doctor had ever asked me that. Ever.

The fact that allopathic doctors didn't and to this day still don't ask us what we're eating made me wonder why the focus is always solidly on pharmaceuticals and not on food. I decided to do a little research to help you understand further why you get what you get when you see an allopathic physician.

I learned from websites like www.onegreenplanet.org and www.in-training.org that billions of dollars are paid to doctors, universities and even to the FDA (Food and Drug Administration). This is the same FDA that's supposed to be watching out for our health and well being. These billions are reportedly paid by the pharmaceutical companies to influence the teaching of medical students in favor of the drug companies.

Many medical students have no idea how much influence pharmaceutical companies have on their education. As reported in the New York Times, there was significant concern voiced by a group of students in 2009 at the Harvard Medical School. The students' concern was that the pharmaceutical industry scandals, criminal convictions, fines and proven cherry picking in research and drug trials had put the medical profession in a very bad light. One student even discovered that a full time professor who had touted the benefits of cholesterol medication and had pushed aside a student's question about the drug's side effects was actually a paid consultant to 10 drug companies.

It's no wonder, with the strong influence of the pharmaceutical companies, that there is no focus on nutrition. Very simply, where is the profit if you eat to be well? If you eat to be well, you won't be as likely to get in line for the myriad of drugs developed to suppress the symptoms caused by our Standard American Diet!

Here's another question for you: how qualified are allopathic physicians to advise us on our diets? How many hours of nutrition training does the average medical student have to take during their studies? I began to wonder about this and did some research into that subject. What I found astounded me, but when I paired it with the influence Big Pharma has on the medical teaching schools, it made perfect sense.

"Today, most medical schools in the United States teach less than 25 hours of nutrition over four years. The fact that less than 20 percent of medical schools have a single required course in nutrition, it's a scandal. It's outrageous. It's obscene," David Eisenberg, adjunct associate professor of nutrition at Harvard T. H. Chan School of Public Health, said in an interview with PBS NewsHour in May of 2017.

The fact that this continues to be the case in spite of the known connection between diet and many preventable diseases I feel is unbelievably irresponsible. For me, this included the connection between diet and chronic depression.

Rather than help me understand the connection between what I was eating and decades of struggling with a mental disability that could have been cured by changing my eating habits, the ability to cure my depression was hidden from me. Instead, I was prescribed drugs that did nothing to cure my depression but only enriched those at the other end of the prescription pad, and I'm not just blaming the doctors with this statement.

I don't know about you, but this makes me really angry! Our health is being put at risk for financial profit, and it's not only about depression. What about diabetes, arthritis, cancer, autoimmune diseases and more that are affected by inflammatory foods?

Some young medical students are aware and are protesting, but there is no mandated standard for education regarding nutrition. Each medical school is allowed to teach what and as much as they wish in this case. Some schools are offering online courses sometimes called "healthy kitchen" programs, but there is no requirement to obtain a basic knowledge of healthy nutrition in order to become a licensed allopathic physician.

Doesn't it make sense that if our traditional doctors understood food and the effect it has on our bodies and on our health, the discussion and the process of assessing what is wrong when we have a health issue would be very different?

Simply from a logical way of thinking, I can't understand how it makes more sense to isolate the different organs and functions from one another and treat them individually than it does to look at the total body all together with each organ affecting the others and all working together. Unless you are not human, the answer is that your organs all function together.

That is a wonderful segue into talking about Functional Medicine, but before I do, I want to share that personally I found this treatment, this allopathic isolationist approach to the depression that cripples so many people in our society to be completely ineffective. It doesn't create joy in your life, nor does it make you happy, although I can tell you I expected it would. I was told it would take about two weeks for the antidepressant to begin to work, and I counted the days until I would be happy again. It didn't happen. What happened was a dulling of my depression so I could function better.

The treatment didn't alleviate my depression though...it was still there. It also gave me a host of other symptoms including a muddled mind that couldn't think clearly. That was a constant frustration for me. I didn't feel like myself either, which is odd to write about as a negative, as feeling like myself was being depressed. It's difficult to describe, but I didn't feel like the essence of me anymore. If you've struggled with depression perhaps that will make sense to you in some way.

Where Allopathic Medicine works to suppress symptoms of illness, Functional Medicine seeks to discover the *cause of the disease or condition* rather than to suppress the symptoms of the disease or condition. Functional Medicine looks at the body as a whole and tries to get to the root of the disease or condition, often times with diet. For example, if the condition is joint pain, the functional medicine practitioner will look at the patient's diet to determine what foods might be causing the symptoms of joint pain. If the condition is depression, the functional medicine practitioner will look at diet, surroundings, environmental toxins, etc. to which the patient is exposed to determine what might be causing the depression in the first place. The unbelievable upside to this is that rather than continuing to live with depression symptoms that are just dulled by anti-depressant drugs, the root cause can many times be uncovered, managed or eliminated, and the result can be real relief from the struggles of living with depression.

When you approach any disease or condition with Functional Medicine, the odds are great that other benefits will be enjoyed. Looking at the body as a whole gives you tremendous power and control over how you feel both mentally and physically as well as, believe it or not, control over your weight!

I was always struck by my mother's doctors here in Massachusetts who were traditional practitioners of Allopathic Medicine and who were often extremely unhealthy looking. Several of them were very overweight, flushed in appearance, puffy faced; they just didn't look healthy. Take a look at functional medicine practitioners like Dr. Mark Hyman, Dr. Joel Fuhrman and Dr. Neal Barnard. They are lean and trim with no puffiness in their faces. There is a reason for that. They practice what they preach, which is how to eat to be well. We'll discuss more about that in the pages ahead.

As we move forward, it's important to reiterate that Functional Medicine seeks to discover the *cause of the disease or condition* rather than to *suppress the symptoms* of the disease or condition. Functional Medicine looks at the body as a whole and tries to get to the root of the disease or condition, often times with diet. By the way, you don't have to be struggling with a disease to benefit from the teachings of functional medicine.

Now that you know the two roads you can travel down when you're seeking to "disappear" depression, let's talk about what usually happens when you realize you are depressed and seek help in our medical world today.

CHAPTER FIVE

What is the Process When You Realize You are Depressed?

"What the caterpillar calls the end of the world, the master calls a butterfly."

~Richard Bach

I remember sitting on our deck with Rob one summer afternoon many years ago. I remember it was a few years after my younger sister had passed away, and he suddenly asked me, "Aren't you tired of being depressed?" I thought I was fooling the world, but it's hard to fool those closest to you who know you so well. It was hard for me to acknowledge that it was tough for Rob to live with someone who was depressed and struggling with her mood all the time.

When you decide to get help and go the regular Allopathic route, often it's a two or three step process unless you go to a psychiatrist right away. The way insurance usually works, you first need to see your primary care physician, who sends you to an LICSW (Licensed Independent Clinical Social Worker) to get the official word on what you know already; yes, you are depressed. Then you are referred to the man (or woman) with the prescription pad who will "save you" from your depression.

I decided to call my doctor and begin the process he offered me which was the only route to the anti-depressants I hoped would be a chance for me to feel better. I had to talk to an LICSW who said yes, I was depressed. He then referred me to a psychiatrist who was the keeper of the prescription pad. I was excited and very hopeful once I made the decision to seek help. I just knew the drugs would make me feel happy. They told me it would take at least two weeks for the antidepressants to do their thing. Ok. Then I would feel happy. I couldn't wait to feel better.

They put me on some drug; honestly, I forget which one. It might have been Prosac. Whatever it was, it didn't work, so they put me on Zoloft. Remember that if these drugs are going to modify your mood and behavior, it takes 2-3 weeks to do so, so your misery hangs on for a while, but you have your eye firmly fixed on the end result, and you can't wait to feel better. I remember the anticipation and excitement of feeling happier soon, but antidepressants don't make you feel happy. What they do is dull the pain of your depression and sort of level you off so you don't feel quite so badly depressed in most cases.

I eventually started to feel a bit less depressed on the Zoloft, and then my father died. Suddenly I was depressed again. As my doctor put it, I "crashed on Zoloft". On to the next medication which was Paxil. This worked better, and I was on that for several years until I began to notice I didn't feel quite "right". I felt muddy in my head. It took a while to realize this, because not being as sad and getting a good night's sleep was such a welcome relief.

Chapter Six

Antidepressants - Expected Side Effects and How They Affected Me

"Before you treat a man with a condition, know that not all cures can heal all people. For the chemistry that works on one patient may not work for the next, because even medicine has its own conditions."

~Suzy Kassem

Side Effects of Antidepressants

All prescription drugs come with side effects. The ads on TV usually play happy music while they tell you that you can have a stroke or die from whatever drug they're promoting. Try watching the ads without the sound. It's very entertaining to watch the people sad and struggling until they get the drug of the moment. The angst on the faces of the actors and the relief and joy once they take the drug are really something!

The side effects of anti-depressants as reported by the Mayo Clinic, Harvard Medical School and other medical communities are many and include:

- increased appetite and weight gain
- loss of sexual desire and other sexual problems, such as erectile dysfunction and decreased orgasm
- fatigue and drowsiness

- nausea
- insomnia
- dry mouth
- blurred vision
- constipation
- dizziness
- agitation
- irritability
- anxiety
- thoughts of suicide

While I was researching this section of the book, I came across this warning about a depression medication. I'm including it without edits as I found it online so you can see the extent of the side effects. (Whatever medications you are currently taking whether for depression or for another condition, I strongly urge you to check online for side effects just to inform yourself.)

Information for one depression medication:

Please see **FULL PRESCRIBING INFORMATION**, including **BOXED WARNING**, and Medication Guide for **REXULTI**.
INDICATION AND IMPORTANT SAFETY INFORMATION for REXULTI
INDICATION: REXULTI is a prescription medicine used to treat:

- Major depressive disorder (MDD): REXULTI is used with antidepressant medicines, when your healthcare provider determines that an antidepressant alone is not enough to treat your depression.

It is not known if REXULTI is safe and effective in people under 18 years of age.

IMPORTANT SAFETY INFORMATION:
Medicines like REXULTI can raise the risk of death in elderly people who have lost touch with reality (psychosis) due to

confusion and memory loss (dementia). REXULTI is not approved for treating patients with dementia-related psychosis. Antidepressants may increase suicidal thoughts or actions in some children, teenagers, or young adults within the first few months of treatment. Pay close attention to any changes, especially sudden changes in mood, behaviors, thoughts, or feelings and report such changes to the healthcare provider. This is very important when antidepressant medicine is started or when the dose is changed. REXULTI is approved only for adults 18 and over with depression.

Tell your healthcare provider right away if you have some or all of the following serious side effects:

- **Stroke in elderly people (cerebrovascular problems) that can lead to death.**
- **Neuroleptic Malignant Syndrome (NMS):** high fever, stiff muscles, confusion, sweating, changes in pulse, heart rate, and blood pressure as these may be symptoms of a rare but potentially fatal condition.
- **Uncontrolled body movements** in your face, tongue or other body parts **(tardive dyskinesia, TD)**. TD may become permanent, and may start after you stop taking REXULTI.
- **Problems with your metabolism: High blood sugar (hyperglycemia).** If you have diabetes or risk factors for it, your healthcare provider should monitor your blood sugar.
- **Increased fat levels (cholesterol and triglycerides) in your blood or weight gain.**
- **Low white blood cell count.**
- **Decreased blood pressure** (orthostatic hypotension).
- **Seizures** (convulsions).
- **Problems controlling your body temperature so that you feel too warm.** Avoid getting overheated or dehydrated while taking REXULTI.

- **Difficulty swallowing that can cause food or liquid to get into your lungs.**

The **most common side effects** of REXULTI include weight gain and an inner sense of restlessness such as feeling like you need to move. These are not all the possible side effects of REXULTI. Tell your doctor about all the medicines you're taking, since there are some risks for drug interaction. Until you know how REXULTI affects you, do not drive, operate machinery or do dangerous activities. REXULTI may make you feel drowsy. Avoid drinking alcohol while taking REXULTI.

I hope you read that in detail. If you had the option of taking a drug like this with all the possible side effects, or changing how you eat to alleviate your symptoms, what would you do? Wouldn't you rather change what you eat than risk all this? If the answer is "no", I don't understand.

Personally, I made the decision to get off Paxil. In fact, I was on and off Paxil at least three times. Each time I went on it because I couldn't stand trying to live and function being so depressed all the time. Then I got off it, because I couldn't stand how I felt, and I couldn't tolerate the side effects of the drug.

Each time I stopped taking the antidepressant gradually, and I did so with my doctor's guidance. It's crucial when you stop taking these drugs to get off them *very carefully under your doctor's supervision.* There are side effects you experience when you are taking them and side effects when you try to stop taking them. Especially if you have taken anti-depressants for a very long time, they can be addictive and very difficult to stop.

If and when you do decide to get off this medication, expect to feel dizzy and disoriented for a while. These drugs can be scary, and I can't stress enough that you have to be very, very careful.

CHAPTER SEVEN

What about Natural Treatments for Depression?

"I will be stronger than my sadness."
~ Jasmine Warga

When I realized I couldn't tolerate the side effects of the Paxil, I researched and tried alternative methods. I put myself on St. John's Wort for a time. There are differing reports on the effectiveness of this herbal substance, and studies in Europe have reported positive results. I honestly don't think it helped me very much, but my determination to feel better without pharmaceuticals spurred me onward. I tried to incorporate exercise into my regular regimen, but when you're struggling with depression, it's hard to be motivated to move some days. I had days I would be so debilitated, I would literally sit at my desk with my head in my hands and just wait for time to pass. Not a good way to spend your life.

I struggled ahead with this protocol for a while and maintained adequately. Then my mom was diagnosed with dementia. Her dementia was propelled forward by a series of strokes, and I had to move her from her home of more than fifty years, where I had grown up, into an assisted living facility. She was there for two weeks and suffered a major stroke which forced another move... this time to the memory loss section. My mom had been so sharp that this change was very hard to watch; I know it was even harder for her as she was occasionally still with it enough to realize she couldn't find the right words to communicate any longer. It would make her so frustrated. "That makes me so mad!" she would say when she couldn't think of the words she wanted. She also often thought she was back in New Jersey where she grew up, that her mother was still alive and she often called me by her sister's name, Gladys. For a while it was a good thing to correct her, and then when she got to an advanced stage, it was no longer in her best interest to do so. No reason to upset her. One day when she told me she had dreamed her mother was very ill, I decided it was best to tell her that her mother (who had died 30 years earlier) was not ill. I wasn't lying as she was not ill; she was dead. I made decisions based on what was best for my mom. One afternoon she was cognizant enough to apologize to me. She told me how sorry she was that she was putting me through this. While her sentiment was sincere and so sweet and loving, it made me even sadder and more depressed.

My mom passed away from end stage dementia in September of 2009. I was very tired and emotionally spent. I felt like I had forgotten how to smile. I became more depressed again.

After struggling along for a few months with no improvement, I finally decided to go back on anti-depressants. Back on the Paxil... I was on it for several months, and I did not feel great. Maybe my depression lessened, I honestly don't exactly recall because any benefit was overshadowed by the side effects I experienced. I yawned constantly. I felt like my mind was full of Jello to the point that I was having trouble learning and assimilating information. I wasn't sleeping well and was having vivid, disturbing dreams and nightmares that I couldn't remember once I woke up except for the fact they were very disturbing.

I had dry mouth and waves of nausea that would hit at the most inopportune times. Shopping at the grocery store and smelling prepared food became a real challenge.

Clearly Paxil did not seem to be a good option for me, so I went back to the internet to research side effects. I've learned to go immediately to the fine print. All the side effects I was experiencing were listed there, and so I had to get off the Paxil again. I accomplished that, but I didn't know where to turn next. There were two tools that seemed to make a difference for me during that time.

The first was SAMe or S-Adenosyl Methionine. I had read it assists with mood and brain function, so I decided to begin taking it to see if that would help me at all. SAMe is a chemical found naturally in the body. This fact alone made it much more attractive to me than the prescription medications I had been on and off for years with their unpleasant side effects. SAMe has additional benefits in that it's beneficial for your joint health and also supports your liver where the SAMe your body makes is produced. Specifically, SAMe supports joint strength, liver detoxification, mood and brain function. Excellent! I liked that very much, and I could swear I felt a little bit more "up" with my mood about 30 – 40 minutes after taking it.

At the same time, I had been reading about SAD (Seasonal Affective Disorder). I suspected it was part of my depression struggle as I had always had a dread of the approaching fall season. It made me feel depressed just knowing it was looming. As I said earlier, I grew up and have always lived in the Northeast, so the flowers would be dying and freezing, and the light changed greatly. The light in my bedroom in the home in which I grew up would change and used to depress me terribly as a teenager. The fall shadows were such a downer for me.

I had read about full spectrum light therapy and decided to try it. Full spectrum light units give off light that is similar in color composition to natural daylight, and my personal experience using them was really good. It used to be that you had to buy a huge bank of full spectrum lights which were very expensive and bulky. Now they have small, portable units you can carry with you, so in winter months you can have it on your desk at the office or at home and enjoy the benefit while you work.

I decided to order myself a full spectrum light and to give that a try. I found one that I could hang on the top of my laptop which I used a good part of the day. The last year I struggled with depression, the combination of SAMe and the full spectrum light unit during the fall and winter months helped me quite a bit. In fact, I made it through that winter in better shape than I could remember for a very long time.

Concurrent with these changes, Rob realized he was having intense side effects from the statin drug he was taking, so we decided to drastically change how we eat to improve his cholesterol readings and get him off the statin. (Now we'll go back to the beginning of this story when we began to change how and what we eat...)

Section III

An Accidental Miracle

Life is a matter of choices, and
every choice you make makes you.

~John C. Maxwell

While this quote is so true, the amazing part of this story is that I didn't make conscious choices to improve my mental health.

Now I understand what I did was completely by accident, and now I make conscious choices going forward.

How lucky was I??

CHAPTER EIGHT
The Journey Begins

"Yesterday I was clever, so I wanted to change the world. Today I am wise, so I am changing myself."

~ Rumi

I hate to cook! Or at least I did. Now I love it, but back in the day not so much, and I was awful at it! I mean really, *really* bad! At home growing up, I was allowed to set the table and clean up after. Not trusted to watch the stove at all. I had no interest, no focus and would inevitably forget and burn the food while my mom was picking my dad up at the train station (that was in the days of one car per family).

Another time, when I was grown and in my own apartment, I put green beans on to cook. For me at the time, this meant simmering them on the stove in water only and cooking them until they were grey. I went to the grocery store, which was five minutes around the corner, to get something I needed for dinner. I completely forgot the beans and decided to do a major shopping. By the time I got home, my apartment was full of smoke. Fortunately, I didn't burn down the building.

Where I am now with cooking is that I really enjoy it! I think part of the shift is that I like the food I eat now while the food I used to eat didn't excite me. It wasn't very interesting, and I never liked eating meat. Don't misunderstand and assume I am judging you if you do. For me, I didn't like the taste or the texture. I never did. I also like roasted or sautéed veggies rather than boiled or steamed. I like spices and flavors that compliment the food. It's interesting to try out different combinations. I find cooking relaxing and fun now.

I share this so those of you who think you can't cook will have renewed interest and hope. Please believe me when I say, and I say this with conviction: "If I can do it, you can do it!" Honestly, when you're creating food that you love and that makes you feel so much better, it's a great experience!

As an aside, it's because of this transformational experience that I've begun to incorporate teaching how to cook the whole healthy food I now eat into my TV show, "Thin Strong Healthy" and into the short videos I post on my YouTube channel. The way I cook is not difficult; it's simple and delicious. I've learned that when you eat healthy food that's interesting and easily prepared, you'll lose more than just depression. You'll drop weight without dieting, and you can enjoy more normal glucose levels and healthier cholesterol levels. Can you imagine not needing to get on the scale or start a diet ever again? It's very possible when you learn to eat this way.

I went from burned beans to a TV show. Again, if I can do it, you can do it!

But we'll get back to this a little later.

My journey to recovery from chronic depression began as a complete accident when my husband, Rob, began having some very disturbing health issues and apparent side effects. We eventually realized they were tied to a widely prescribed cholesterol lowering drug. He had been on a large dose of the statin drug Lipitor (80 mg/day) and an aspirin regimen for almost seven years as a result of his family history of high cholesterol and heart disease. By the way, cholesterol is *not* your enemy. You need cholesterol to be healthy. It's what happens to our cholesterol from our diet that causes the problems with cholesterol. We'll discuss cholesterol again in Chapter Nine.

Rob had been experiencing severe nerve pain in his abdomen area (neuropathy), weakness in his legs, vivid dreams and nightmares, lack of energy, brain fog and waves of debilitating depression that had become so bad he had begun to feel hopeless about his life and his future. He was having issues with his blood sugar and had been told he was borderline diabetic. His blood glucose levels were so high he had to test his blood sugar twice a day. It was very frightening for us. Vision problems were also coming on with the onset of developing cataracts.

As we began to read about the drugs he was taking (Lipitor and aspirin), we discovered most of his recent health issues appeared to be side effects now listed as possibilities when taking those two drugs, especially the statin, Lipitor. Statins have been widely prescribed for about 20 years, so the problems resulting from their long-term use are only coming to light now.

Rob was determined to get off the medication that seemed to be slowly killing him. That meant we had to get his cholesterol and his blood sugar under control without drugs, so he began to change his diet. To support him, and because I do most of the food preparation in our house, I joined his efforts. Our mantra became, "Our food is our medicine".

Where to begin and how to begin...

For anyone wanting to follow this path, I strongly suggest you begin at home where you can control what you're eating with no judgment or questions from others; at least until you get a sense of what you're doing. You'd be amazed at the peer pressure to eat the Standard American Diet without question.

We began with a huge cleanout. We purged our refrigerator and our pantry. Everything in a box went; everything with preservatives went; everything processed went. No more frozen pre-prepared foods either. We donated a lot of food that was fine date-wise, but which we felt was no longer in our best interest to eat.

We began by eating very simply. Lots of salads, and I don't mean just boring lettuce, tomatoes and cucumbers! We added beets and seeds, olives and celery, endive and peppers, carrots and capers. We changed our lettuce from iceberg to organic green and red leaf lettuce. We shopped clutching the list of the Clean Fifteen and the Dirty Dozen from the Environmental Working Group (EWG.org) to guide us and to help us stay within a reasonable budget for our healthy new diet. I'll explain this list in greater detail later in this chapter in the section titled, "Labels and Lists and Learning".

We rather arrogantly thought we crushed it right out of the gate, and to a great extent, we did. We got a really good start by cranking our food back to very simple. What we found, however, was that there was so much more to learn. Do you choose Xanthan Gum or Guar Gum? What kind of sweetener doesn't give you a glucose bump if you must use a sweetener? What are ways to keep cooking simple but crank up the flavor with spices, different oils and seasonings? What kind of chocolate is best if you need a chocolate fix? It's been a process, and it's one that is ongoing.

We read labels...everything with sugar, wheat, dairy, trans fats, preservatives, chemicals we couldn't pronounce went...all gone!

We had been eating a lot of processed foods including a lot of soy. Looking into this made us aware of GMOs (genetically modified organisms) and that whole can of worms. So, soy was gone; my much loved "fakin' bacon" made of soy, my sausages made of soy, and my soy breakfast sausage patties all went buh-buy.

Love corn on the cob? I did. Corn is a tough subject when you're talking eating "clean". Corn by-products are in so many food items, but corn is a victim of GMO, and corn is also very high in sugar and carbohydrate. If blood sugar control is not a major issue for you, then you should still be concerned and aware of the ancestry of the corn you choose to eat. Is it organic, or could it be GMO corn? Knowing what I know now, I would never eat corn that isn't organic.

You may be wondering what was left to eat. So were we, but we weren't done eliminating foods from our list of items we would put on our plates yet.

Sugar went. My beloved Peanut M&Ms that I could (and did at one time) eat by the relatively large bagful...gone. I used to joke using a line from the 70s show, "Rhoda". She said about candy, and I'm paraphrasing here..."I don't know why I'm eating this; I should just apply it directly to my hips!" At one time, I packed on more than a few pounds courtesy of Peanut M&Ms.

"Eat to live, don't live to eat!"

~Benjamin Franklin

I've tried to determine who said this, and although it's been attributed to a number of famous people throughout history, most give credit for it to Benjamin Franklin, so for our purposes here, I'll give Ben the credit.

It doesn't matter who said it; it's brilliant, and is a perfect introduction to a couple of suggestions regarding portion control and eating in moderation.

I'm a big fan of using a smaller plate for your meals. There's a lot to be said for visual satisfaction with food. If food looks delicious, regardless of how it actually tastes, you'll be more interested in eating it than if it doesn't look appealing. By that same token, if you have the portions of food you want to eat on a large plate and they look lost, you'll be inclined to think you'll still be hungry once you finish and will want more food. If the portions fill a smaller plate, you'll most likely not have that same thought. Some of this is quite frankly playing games with your mind. Eating and appetite are influenced by your mind and by your perception of the food you are about to eat.

The next suggestion is to begin to enjoy feeling a little bit hungry. Not starving, but a little bit hungry. It's a tough thing to convey, but it's a good practice to incorporate. When you eat a meal, it's in your best interest to push away from the table before you are completely full and certainly before you are stuffed. I know some people eat and eat and never feel full, and it's not their fault. It's the fault of their hunger hormones not behaving, and we'll talk more about this later in the section on Hunger Hormones and Gut Health in Chapter Eleven. I want to stress though, that so much of the battle with food, eating and weight is *not your fault!*

Eating out can be a challenge as the portions can be easily enough for two meals! Here's an easy thing you can do though. When your meal arrives, ask your server for a to-go container, and divide your meal in half before you begin to eat. If you do this, you're not even tempted to eat the whole thing. You'll eat a moderate portion of everything and will still have a way to enjoy it again for your next lunch or dinner. I wish I could claim this as an original idea, but my friend Joan told me about this one. I thought it was a great idea!

I strongly suggest you cozy up to the idea of not feeling stuffed, dare I say not even completely full. You don't want to be starving though. That's certainly not in your best interest as the odds are if you get really hungry, you will be more likely to lose self control and reach for the nearest bag of sugar and carbs in the form of cookies or chips. Just be aware of how full you feel. Unconscious eating to the point of feeling stuffed has gotten us into a lot of trouble with our weight and consequently with our health.

Just be aware. *Eat mindfully*, and observe when you are no longer hungry. Experiment pushing away from your food at this point and notice if you feel satisfied fifteen or twenty minutes later when your brain has gotten the message that Yes! You are full!

Our Own Personal Eating Revolution

We began by reading as much as we could on the subject of healthy eating, and we were very fortunate to hear a program or two on PBS that influenced our journey and helped us get a really good start. The first life changing program featured Dr. Mark Hyman who at the time was a practitioner of functional medicine here in Massachusetts. We bought his book, "The Blood Sugar Solution" and began our new clean-eating adventure.

"The power of community to create health is far greater than any physician, clinic or hospital."

~ Dr. Mark Hyman

Dr. Hyman advocates addressing the root causes of chronic illness by using the principles of functional medicine. He teaches the merits of learning to stop managing symptoms and instead treating the underlying causes of those symptoms by changing what and how we eat and what we are exposed to in our daily lives.

There have been many others who have provided education and have lighted our path during the years we have spent reinventing our health through better nutrition. Dr. Hyman was the first one we discovered, and so it's important to me that I highlight his contribution to my personal freedom from depression. Someday I hope to meet him in person to thank him for being the catalyst for my new life. Until then...Thank you Dr. Hyman!

Bye-bye dairy

Dairy products contain lactose in varying degrees depending upon the product. They elicit a high insulin response although they can be low in carbohydrate content and have a low glycemic index, that is, they are slower to affect the blood glucose level.

Many people are allergic or sensitive to dairy, so one of the decisions we made was to eliminate dairy. No more milk, yogurt or cheese. Giving up cheese was a hard one for me. I love cheese, but not enough to want to risk being depressed again.

By the way, these days I occasionally eat cheese. Organic or from grass fed cows and in condiment sized servings. No more slab of cheese as the protein of the meal which I did do at one time.

As an aside, did you know that if you are trying to get beneficial bacteria from eating yogurt, you should not eat it with either table sugar or with fruit sugar as it inactivates the bacteria? It would be nice to know this fact before you spend money on the healthiest yogurt you can find that contains fruit and sugar. When it comes to your food supply, you can never let your guard down. Read books, question and always, always read your food labels. Even if you consistently choose a certain food you have vetted in the past, they may change the ingredients. It happens frequently, and unfortunately, they don't often change the ingredients for the better. *Always read your food labels!*

We'll come back to dairy later on when we discuss inflammation, but for now, let's move on to gluten.

White Flour and Gluten

Closely following dairy was white flour and gluten and all the many, many food products that contain gluten. Did you know McDonald's sprays their French fries with gluten? Why would they do that? The answer is that gluten is a highly addictive substance! Ever wonder why you crave certain "easy" fast foods? Maybe you crave them and you notice you're not really hungry even though you're craving them. Now you know why. Fast food and other genres of processed foods are engineered to be addictive to keep you coming back for more. It really is diabolical on the part of the big food industry. An additional fact of which to be aware is that the wheat in our country has been engineered to be higher in gluten content as well as shorter in height and faster growing. The wheat we have access to in our current food supply is not the same wheat as our great grandparents ate. We'll discuss gluten again in Chapter Twelve when we talk about Gluten and Inflammation.

Labels and Lists and Learning

To have the chance to be healthy in the long term, we all need to take a hard line with ourselves and our diets. We need to make what are sometimes difficult, but really good, healthy decisions for ourselves.

Rob and I looked at *all natural* foods until we discovered that "all natural" means nothing as far as the quality and healthfulness of the food is concerned. It could be "all-natural" bad stuff like all natural GMO corn, all natural sugar, all natural corn syrup, all natural poison... "all natural" has come to mean absolutely nothing good that you can rely upon to help you eat a healthier diet.

There's no legal definition of "natural", so anyone can say anything. In addition, current regulations allow food manufacturers to claim anything on the *front* of a package of processed food. So, it's just for advertising. That's where they have the chance to grab you with the health buzz word of the day; low fat, low sugar, all natural and so on.

Fortunately, there are laws about what they can and cannot say on the *back* of the package. That's where they have to tell the truth about the product. While this may sound straight forward, it's not. We'll talk more about how to read labels in a bit.

We became label readers. We learned to go right to the back of the package and try to sort out what was really in the food we contemplated buying.

We were very fortunate one day, early on in our adventure, to meet a woman in a Trader Joe's produce department who overheard us trying to make good choices. She asked if we knew about the Dirty Dozen and the Clean 15. We said did not! She was kind enough to let us take a photo of her lists, and we have referred to them ever since. These lists are a great place to start, and now I'll pass them on to you. You'll find them in the reference section at the back of this book and also in Chapter Fourteen in the section on Organic vs. Non-Organic.

They were compiled by the Environmental Working Group which has done some amazing work in the field of health and wellness! The EWG updates these lists annually. I encourage you to go to www.ewg.org and download the most recent list. It will guide you as you decide which fruits and veggies must be organic and which are safer conventional ones to purchase and eat.

We learned that not all fat is bad fat! Who knew? The low fat/no fat craze of the 1990s did our brains and our bodies great harm by demonizing all fat.

Our brains are more than 60% fat, so when we deny our brain a basic component it needs to stay healthy, good fat, we do not help ourselves at all. In fact, the low-fat diet craze created an aging population riddled with dementia, Alzheimer's and general declining brain health.

It's not fat in general, but the type of fat that is important. The type of fat found in processed foods is the real boogie man in our health as far as fat is concerned, and we'll discuss the different types of fat in greater detail in Chapter Twelve. For now, just be aware that our brains need good healthy fat to stay young and supple.

CHAPTER NINE

It's the Inflammation, Stupid!

"...depression is just a label we give to that collection of symptoms. It tells you nothing about what caused the symptoms."

~Dr. Mark Hyman

When something wonderful happens to you that is a complete mystery... in my case a life miracle... and you have no understanding of how that miracle occurred, you really want to learn what happened so you don't undo the goodness. That's how I came to do what I'm doing now with writing, coaching, speaking and teaching about healthy eating.

Don't misunderstand me, I knew changing how I ate affected the miracle, but was it getting off sugar or wheat and gluten that did it? Was it not eating processed foods and all the chemicals and preservatives? Was it eliminating dairy? Was it changing my shampoos and personal care products and getting rid of sodium laurel sulfate and sodium laureth sulfate? What was it that made such a difference and "disappeared" my decades of depression and has kept it gone for more than five years?

It was important for me to understand what had happened so I would never go back to living in that darkness again. If you struggle with depression, imagine for just a minute having that dark cloud gone. I mean really gone! Imagine feeling confident every day and trusting you won't have to wonder if depression will find you again.

It took me several years to put the pieces together and to connect the dots about what had ended my depression. So for years I wondered what I had eliminated from my diet that had made the difference.

I was pretty sure sugar had something to do with it. When I was 28, I was diagnosed as having severe hypoglycemia, which is low blood sugar (as opposed to hyperglycemia or diabetes where your sugar levels are too high). I was on a strict diet after that diagnosis. No sugar, coffee, alcohol or white flour for a year. At the time, I didn't know sugar was everywhere and in everything. There were so many different names of sugar. (See Chapter Eleven for an alphabetical list of over *sixty* names of sugar!) Honey was natural; wasn't that ok? Also, I didn't know at the time so many foods I thought (or was told) were ok to eat converted to sugar very quickly once I ate them. Some began converting to sugar while I was still chewing them!

I knew I was sensitive to wheat and dairy, so was that what made the difference?

For years I wondered but was too afraid of becoming depressed again to experiment and find out.

What I didn't know was the connection between your gut and your brain. One day earlier this year, I read a post written by Dr. Kelly Brogan. Dr. Brogan is a women's psychiatrist who practices in Manhattan. Schooled in the traditional allopathic way, she began to question traditional medicine and eventually veered off course into a more functional way of practicing psychiatry. In the post I read, she discussed the connection between the gut and the brain and how the brain doesn't feel pain. Sure you get a headache, but that's not in your brain like a stomach ache is in your gut. She explained the inflammation that occurs in your gut is telegraphed to your brain via the vagus nerve. Your brain is experiencing inflammation, but not a "brainache", so you don't know your brain is struggling with inflammation the same way a food you may be sensitive to would upset your stomach. The fact is that *inflammation in your brain manifests as depression!*

When I heard this, the light bulb turned on for me! The pieces of the puzzle I had been assembling finally began to fit together and make sense. Without realizing it, I had been eating a low inflammatory diet for the past five years! It wasn't the individual types of food that I was or wasn't eating; it was the sum total of the foods I had been eating. I had simply reduced the inflammation in my body and in my brain thus alleviating my depression.

This was hugely empowering! Not just for me, but for my mission to help others relieve their depression and live healthier, happier lives.

Inflammation and Cholesterol

While we're on the subject of inflammation, let's talk a bit about cholesterol which, by the way, is not a bad thing. Cholesterol is not your enemy; cholesterol is your friend. In fact, you need cholesterol. Before you think I've totally lost it, allow me to explain.

Why do you need cholesterol? Cholesterol is found in every cell of your body. You need it to produce hormones, vitamin D, bile acids that help you digest your food, and you need it to produce cell membranes. Cholesterol is a soft waxy substance that is found in every cell as well as in our bloodstream, and it is *vital* for a healthy brain.

Traditional teaching tells us there are two types of cholesterol. HDL is known as the "good" cholesterol while LDL is known as the "bad" cholesterol. That's a good start, but it's an overly simplistic explanation. It's quite a bit more complicated than that, doesn't tell the full story and makes the bad guy out of LDL which is not always the case.

HDL or high-density lipoprotein is believed to help prevent heart disease which is why it is beneficial to have your HDL levels high. HDL helps remove any excess cholesterol from arterial plaque in our arteries, and that's a good thing.

LDL or low-density lipoprotein is demonized because it is widely believed it may build up in your arteries forming plaque on the arterial walls. Our cholesterol tests most often call out our HDL and LDL levels. What is missing in these test results is the fact that there are different kinds of LDL cholesterol. For our purposes, we'll simplify a complex discussion and say there is large LDL and small LDL.

So, how is cholesterol related to inflammation? Very simply, not all LDL cholesterol is bad cholesterol. It's actually our highly inflammatory American diet of too much sugar, too many processed grains and foods, our sedentary lifestyles, etc. that cause inflammation in our bodies to change our LDL cholesterol from its original soft fluffy buoyant (large) character to a hard dense (small) LDL cholesterol. It's this hard dense LDL that attaches to the artery walls forming plaque and causing the inflammation that promotes cardiovascular disease. This plaque makes our arteries narrow and causes them to become less flexible. If a clot forms in one of these compromised arteries and makes it to your heart or your brain, the likelihood that you will suffer a heart attack or a stroke is significant.

Inflammation is the enemy. So, once again, it's the inflammation; and once again, it's all connected!

I could have simply written "it's the inflammation; it's all connected"...the end. It really is that simple!

CHAPTER TEN

So what is a low inflammatory diet?

"Let food be thy medicine and medicine be thy food."

~ Hippocrates

Surprisingly enough, a low inflammatory diet is something most of us have heard of. It's not complicated. In fact, it's so simple that in our processed food world, it is confusing and hard to achieve.

Time for my annual "New Year rant" if you will indulge me. There are so many diets on the market. Watching TV in January makes me crazy because of all the diet gimmicks. There are so many programs that are advertised after the holidays when many of us have gained excess weight because we ate things we shouldn't have, and we ate too much of them!

The burning question I always have is, what happens when you've lost the weight by eating the food you've purchased from XYZ diet company and then you go off their program and stop eating their food? The answer is, more often than not, that you will gain back the weight you lost, and often you will gain back even more weight than you lost. This feeds into the yo-yo dieting that so many people experience during their weight loss struggles. Doesn't it make sense to learn how to eat to support your long term health instead? To learn to eat to stay and be well, to help your body find its own perfect weight and to provide your body the nutrients it needs to heal itself of struggle and disease? To learn to eat to stave off chronic diseases associated with aging so you enjoy health and vitality until the very last days of your time here? I would rather see people spend money wisely on healthy food than on a diet program that will ultimately take their money and let them down.

Your body is a perfect machine. If you give it the fuel it needs, it will treat you well. If you give it what approximates gasoline with water in it, you will never enjoy a smooth ride no matter what diet plans you try or what supplements you take.

A low inflammatory diet consists of food; real whole food! What do I mean by whole food? I'm referring to unprocessed fruits and vegetables for the major portion of what you eat. If you eat meat, look for pasture raised meat and poultry, and wild caught fish. Whole unprocessed grains are also on the menu. What a low inflammatory diet is not is fast food and food that has been so processed it's unrecognizable, devoid of its original nutritional value so it must then be "revitalized" with minerals and a vitamin or two so Big Food can advertise the benefits loudly on the front of the package. Real whole food is not food that has had all the fat removed (taking the flavor with it) and then "flavored-up" with gobs of salt and sugar. Check your food labels on your no-fat and low-fat "foods" for the amount of salt and sugar if you doubt me.

Again...it's simple.

Let's talk about the worst place to carry extra weight. Have you heard of visceral fat or belly fat?

Visceral Fat and Why We are So Overweight

Do you ever wonder why we as a nation are so frighteningly overweight? Let me begin by saying, "It's not your fault". If you struggle with your weight, it's not your fault. It's not your fault you spend money on diet foods and diet programs that promise you the moon and may help you lose weight only to let you down while you watch yourself gain back what you lost. As I've said before and as too many of you know from personal experience, most of the time, you gain back more weight than you lost in the first place.

You eat less, you exercise more and you still gain weight. Women in their 40s and 50s think it's hormonal and their metabolism is just slowing down. The weight gain is inevitable; get used to it.

Not true! Of course portion control comes into play, and regular exercise is important for all of us for many reasons, but more importantly, it's *what you eat* that makes you or breaks you weight-wise and health-wise.

Many of us carry weight in our bulging hips and thighs (mostly for women, that is), but most of us (men and women) who struggle with weight carry it in our mid-section. Years ago, for you men out there, this was referred to as a "beer belly".

Known as visceral fat and commonly referred to as belly fat, this fat is a frighteningly accurate marker for the dangers of developing heart disease, hypertension, dementia, certain types of cancer and rheumatoid arthritis among other chronic diseases. In fact, it's a marker for the inflammatory level of your entire body. Remember, inflammation is the root cause of chronic disease and premature aging. Depression is a disease...a chronic one...and the level of inflammation in your body is a contributor to depression.

It's all connected.

How does insulin fit into the big picture of our struggle with our weight? Insulin is the hormone of fat storage. When we eat foods that trigger the production of insulin, we are indulging in eating habits that are bound to make us fatter and fatter; sicker and sicker. When we eat foods that contain sugar and simple carbohydrates like wheat, the pancreas is notified to get busy and produce insulin to take care of that rising glucose level. If we don't need or burn all the calories we are consuming, not only is our pancreas working extra hard to send out insulin, but any unused calories are stored as new fat cells. Those new fat cells all have a blood supply, so your heart works harder to pump blood to the new fat cells.

Foods that raise your blood sugar raise your insulin levels. Increased insulin levels create visceral belly fat. It's not just your belly that gets fat either; your liver gets fat, your intestines get fat, your pancreas and your kidneys get fat. Your heart gets fat as well.

What shape is visceral fat or belly fat? Have you ever thought about that? It's important to visualize this, because I think most of us don't really think about it. Do you assume it sticks out front and sides but is flat inside near your organs? When I see someone who is carrying around a huge "corporation", as my mother used to refer to it, I have to remind myself that this fat is round in shape. It's not sticking out and then flat on the inside of your body. Are you picturing the danger here? Your visceral belly fat is surrounding your organs on the inside of your body.

Because the Standard American Diet (SAD) is loaded with simple processed carbohydrates and sugars, we are on a non-stop bob sled to obesity and diabetes with our food choices.

Your body is a perfect machine. I've said this before, and it bears repeating. If you give it the fuel it needs, it will treat you well. If you give it what approximates gasoline with water in it, you will never enjoy a smooth ride.

Chapter Eleven

How What You Eat Affects You

"It is easier to change a man's religion than to change his diet."
~Margaret Mead

The big question is how do you change your diet? Dieting can be dangerous; you may not be eating the right foods to get all the nutrition you need. What if you begin eating something that has a negative effect on your desired outcome?

The diet industry is huge in this country. Billions are spent yearly by people desperate to lose weight and improve their health. *Did you know Americans spend in excess of $60 billion annually trying to lose weight?*

Making healthy changes with the food choices offered within the typical American diet is a challenge. I speak from experience when I say that you have to be your own advocate and do the work to find out what's best for you. Or just continue reading this book!

Because we are all different and respond differently to various foods, it's your responsibility, through the process of elimination and introduction, to determine which foods are best for you to consume. Choosing to eat whole unprocessed foods is always the best way to eat. Individual sensitivities can be determined to fine-tune your best way of eating.

Although we are all different, when you go out to eat and see people eating widely, ask yourself if they are eating that way because it doesn't negatively affect them or if they are blissfully and unconsciously harming themselves with their food choices?

Dr. David Seaman in his wonderful book, "The Deflame Diet", calls a trip to a fast food restaurant a "drive-by self-shooting." This is because when we eat fast food, we are literally shooting ourselves full of highly inflammatory foods. When we do this, our thought process does not include what foods will support our health, but rather what will taste good and what do we want to eat at that particular moment.

Dr. Seaman goes on to point out that when we are trying to eat a low inflammatory diet, we seem to need direction. What to eat, when to eat it and how much to eat. While this is not a bad thing, and it's good to have a plan (or a diet, if you will) to fall back on and to refer to, it's ironic that when we're loading up on inflammatory foods, we don't need any help. We don't look for direction on what to eat, when to eat it or how much to eat. We just eat and eat until we stuff ourselves.

I have a friend who teases me about how I eat. I worry about her as she is overweight and has had cancer. It never fails that when she's been to the local Chinese restaurant for the buffet take-out, just as she's about to dig in and enjoy it, I come into the kitchen at our work place. One time she just looked up and said, "Oh crap...it's *you!*"

My take-away from this is that I can't be the food police nor can I lecture people when I know they're eating food that harms them. It is all about choice, which is what I told her at the time. I've learned to be a kinder, gentler Cheryl when it comes to what others choose to eat. It *is* all about choice.

Eating out is another challenge. When I'm meeting a friend for a meal, my main request when we're choosing a restaurant is..."As long as I can get a good salad, I'm fine." Honestly though, this means I'm choosing to put myself in the position of knowing I'm almost certainly not eating organic produce. If I choose to put shrimp or salmon on the salad, I will most likely not be eating wild caught fish. I don't eat out often, but when I do, choosing a salad is how I have the most control over what I'm eating.

"Others can stop you temporarily -- you are the only one who can do it permanently."

~Zig Ziglar

It's so simple, it's hard...

The way I've learned to eat to feel so much better and not struggle with depression any longer is very, very simple. In fact, it's so simple that in our world of processed, packaged, fast food, and drive through eating, it's really become quite challenging. Who do you know who steers clear of food in a box, something packaged, who looks for and buys only packaged foods with a maximum of 5 ingredients on the label? Ingredients that you can actually recognize and pronounce? Not too many people I'll bet.

It was documented in Michael Moss' 2014 book "Salt Sugar Fat" that back in 1999 there was a secret meeting of the processed food giants which was held because concern was growing on the part of Pillsbury executives about the increasing weight problem in this country. They were concerned about how fingers were being pointed at the processed food giants much like the tobacco industry had been blamed for the health problems caused by tobacco. Those concerns, once laid out in detail by experts and with data from studies, were quickly squashed by The General Mills executive. He was deemed to be the most powerful person in the room. Michael Moss reports that he said, "Don't talk to me about nutrition. Talk to me about taste, and if this stuff tastes better, don't run around trying to sell stuff that doesn't taste good". Apparently that was the end of the meeting and the end of the processed food giants' concerns about our health and the damage processed food has been doing to us for decades. That meeting was almost 20 years ago. How much thinner were you then? Did you have the same health challenges then that you face now?

You must advocate for yourself and take the time to learn what is best for you to eat to be healthy. It is in your best interest to learn to read food labels!

Let's Talk About Food Labels

Food labels are designed to be confusing. If you stop to read and understand what's in a package of processed food, you may be less apt to purchase and eat it! In addition, checking out the label means you're not simply walking down the aisles in the grocery store tossing "food" in your cart. Instead, you're slowing down to take the time to read what's in the package of food you're contemplating putting in your body.

So, what does the writing on the package really mean? What does it really tell us?

The front of the package is marketing and advertising. Just remember the front is a billboard, and it is *not regulated* by the FDA. You *cannot* depend on the front of the package for facts or for the truth!

The front of many packages loudly proclaims "all natural", "no trans fats", "zero sugar" and so on. Let's address these one by one, so we demystify what sleight of hand is going on here. What trickery is being perpetrated upon us unsuspecting masses?

First of all, "natural" means nothing as far as healthy eating is concerned. *Nothing!* Natural has no legal definition as it pertains to the FDA and to food products. Food labeled "natural", according to the USDA definition does not contain artificial ingredients or preservatives and the ingredients are only minimally processed. However, they may contain antibiotics, growth hormones and other similar chemicals. Products labeled as "natural" may also contain undesirable additives like MSG (monosodium glutamate). MSG causes a whole host of allergic reactions in countless individuals ranging from congestion to migraines to seizures!

When I see "natural" anywhere on a package, it makes me very suspicious about what they're trying to slip by me.

While the front of the package is for advertising, i.e. a billboard, the back of the package is where, by law, they have to tell the truth. Sort of.

What about a package that claims "zero trans fat"? Those words don't necessarily mean the package of food does not contain trans fat. In fact, *federal regulations allow a food label to claim 0 grams of trans fat as long as there is less than half a gram of hydrogenated or partially hydrogenated fat per serving.* So, you may be eating trans fats without realizing it. And what if you eat more than one serving of that food? For example, if one serving actually has .4 g of trans fat but you eat two servings, you've just consumed almost a full gram of trans fat.

Trans fats are found in most processed foods and are often present *even if the nutrition label itself says: Trans Fat 0g.* See the sample nutrition label on the next page, and notice the label indicates *Trans Fat 0 g.* This may or may not be accurate.

Nutrition Facts

8 servings per container

Serving size   2/3 cup (55g)

Amount per serving

Calories   230

	% Daily Value*
Total Fat 8g	**10%**
Saturated Fat 1g	**5%**
Trans Fat 0g	
Cholesterol 0mg	**0%**
Sodium 160mg	**7%**
Total Carbohydrate 37g	**13%**
Dietary Fiber 4g	**14%**
Total Sugars 12g	
Includes 10g Added Sugars	**20%**
Protein 3g	
Vitamin D 2mcg	10%
Calcium 260mg	20%
Iron 8mg	45%
Potassium 235mg	6%

* The % Daily Value (DV) tells you how much a nutrient in a serving of food contributes to a daily diet. 2,000 calories a day is used for general nutrition advice.

To be confident this food truly has no trans fat at all, you'll want to look at the list of ingredients and *read every ingredient* to be sure they haven't slipped trans fats into the product. Even more diabolical, you need to check to see that the portion size isn't something ridiculously small. This is often done to keep the numbers per serving looking good. It follows that if there are hydrogenated or partially hydrogenated oils in the ingredients list, and if the serving size is so ridiculously small that most people would eat at least two servings at one sitting, be aware you are eating significant amounts of trans fat when you thought you were eating **none!**

Check out the sample ingredients list below:

Ingredients: UNBLEACHED ENRICHED FLOUR (WHEAT FLOUR, NIACIN, REDUCED IRON, THIAMINE MONONITRATE {VITAMIN B1}, RIBOFLAVIN {VITAMIN B2}, FOLIC ACID), SOYBEAN OIL, SUGAR, PARTIALLY HYDROGENATED COTTONSEED OIL, SALT, LEAVENING (BAKING SODA AND/OR CALCIUM PHOSPHATE), HIGH FRUCTOSE CORN SYRUP, SOY LECITHIN, MALTED BARLEY ...

Specifically referencing the ingredient label above, cotton isn't a food, so why is it used in processed foods? Most often, the answer lies in profit for big food rather than in what's healthiest for us, the consumers. Cotton oil is cheap, and the majority of consumers don't read ingredient labels, so it's not an issue for the big food companies to use cheap oils that boost their profits and have a longer shelf life because they've been hydrogenated. Also, look at the list of ingredients to see if hydrogenated or partially hydrogenated oils like soy or canola oil are there. These oils are also cheap, so they are used often. They contribute to inflammation however, and it's in your best interest to avoid them.

What about "zero sugar"? Federal regulations also allow a food label to claim 0 g of sugar as long as there is less than half a gram of sugar per serving. If one serving of the food contains less than .5 g of sugar per serving, the amount can be expressed as zero, but if you eat for example, two servings, you have eaten almost a gram of sugar. By the way, 1 g of sugar equals approximately 1/4 teaspoon of sugar.

Also, it's in your best interest to read the list of ingredients to find out if there is sugar disguised as one of the sixty plus names of sugar included in the package of food. Even types of sugar considered natural by many people like honey, maple syrup and agave are still sugar. To your body, sugar is sugar is sugar; your body responds to all of these as it would respond to ordinary table sugar.

Did you know that the recommended daily allowance of sugar for an average weight adult is about twenty five grams or six teaspoons of sugar? *The average American consumes over twenty two teaspoons of sugar per day!*

How does that translate to a can of Classic Coke for example? A twelve ounce can of Coke is one serving, and that one serving contains thirty nine grams of sugar! That translates to nine and three quarter teaspoons of sugar in one can! Keeping in mind that the recommended daily allowance of sugar is six teaspoons, you are well beyond that once you've finished your can of Classic Coke.

What follows is a list in alphabetical order of all the names of sugar you have to be aware of if you want to avoid sugar in your diet:

The Different Names of Sugar

Agave nectar
Barbados sugar
Barley malt
Barley malt syrup
Beet sugar
Brown sugar
Buttered syrup
Cane juice
Cane juice crystals
Cane sugar
Caramel
Carob syrup
Castor sugar
Coconut palm sugar
Coconut sugar
Confectioner's sugar
Corn sweetener
Corn syrup
Corn syrup solids
Date sugar
Dehydrated cane juice
Demerara sugar
Dextran
Dextrin
Dextrose
Diastatic malt
Diatase
Ethyl maltol
Evaporated cane juice
Florida crystals
Free-flowing brown sugars
Fructose Fruit juice
Fruit juice concentrate
Galactose

Glucose
Glucose solids
Golden sugar
Golden syrup
Grape sugar
HFCS (High-Fructose Corn Syrup)
Honey
Honey icing sugar
Icing sugar
Invert sugar
Lactose
Malt sugar
Malt syrup
Maltodextrin
Maltol
Maltose
Mannitol
Mannose
Maple syrup
Molasses
Muscovado
Palm sugar
Panocha
Powdered sugar
Raw sugar
Refiner's syrup
Rice syrup
Saccharose
Sorbitol
Sorghum Syrup
Sucrose Sugar (granulated)
Sweet Sorghum Syrup
Treacle
Turbinado sugar
Yellow sugar

Did you recognize all those names? Some of them I had never even heard of! What *is* treacle for goodness sake?

Can you trust that the serving size listed is realistic? When you're looking at a food label, you have to be very careful about that serving size. Sometimes food manufacturers will list the serving size as ridiculously small so the numbers of salt, sugar, fat and calories look good to you the consumer. They count on you not being aware or not taking the time to fact check what they have indicated on the labels. What is supposed to be "the truth" can be very deceptive.

For example, a serving size of canned soup by a famous soup maker was listed as ¼ cup of soup. I don't know of anyone who would consider a ¼ cup of soup as a real serving, do you? The sodium was so high in this canned soup, that the only way to make the sodium level appear acceptable was to make the serving size ridiculously small.

As with our soup and sodium example, portion size relative to sugar can be deceptive too. For instance, the serving for Oreo cookies is three cookies...three! I don't know about you, but if I were in a frame of mind to break into a box of Oreos, I wouldn't be eating just three. Six, nine, maybe an entire sleeve! That would be more realistic.

Let's talk about the sugar you're getting with just those three Oreos. There are fourteen grams of sugar in just three Oreo cookies. Multiply that by two or three if six or nine will be your serving, and you've just consumed 42 grams of sugar if nine cookies is your serving. That translates to approximately ten and a half teaspoons of sugar, or nearly twice the recommended daily allowance.

While this may not seem so bad, be aware that if you're enjoying your Oreos with your Classic Coke, you're on the fast track to obesity and diabetes.

Cheryl, what do you eat for a treat when you eat the way you do?

Someone asked me this, and it made me think long and hard. The question in its simple form implies that eating fresh whole healthy food isn't a treat, and perhaps the question came from that person's experience where they feel that something sweet or forbidden in some way is a treat. Once I finished pondering this esoteric question, I decided there are two ways to answer.

The first is that you can create healthy versions of most of your favorite "treats".

For example, did you know there are actually healthy versions of ice cream available? In fact, as I write this section, today is National Vanilla Ice Cream Day? It really is! And although I don't often eat dairy these days, I still have it once in a while. The rest of the time, I go to dairy free versions.

We are so fortunate that now there are other ice creams that are really delicious and that don't contain dairy. I'll share with you my current favorite. It's a coconut milk based ice cream, and the vanilla is really good! They call it a non-dairy frozen dessert, but I still call it "ice cream". I like to have it plain, with cut up fresh fruit like blackberries, watermelon and mango or with a little Morecello drizzled over it. Morecello is a blackberry liqueur. You don't need much as it's very potent stuff, but it is packed with flavor and richness!

My point in sharing this with you is that you can still treat yourself with a small serving of something healthy yet delicious when you just really want a dessert or something sweet. Your taste buds will adjust once you're off sugar for a while too, and you won't need the intense sweetness of processed sugar to feel satisfied with your craving for a treat.

This particular ice cream that's my favorite is sweetened with monk fruit, and only has 1 gram of sugar per serving!

Instead of the sweetness of sugar hitting your tongue, you will be more aware of the vanilla flavor.

It comes in other flavors as well; chocolate, mint chocolate chip and butter pecan. I usually keep a pint of vanilla and chocolate in the freezer as it makes a quick treat or an easy dessert when we have company over for dinner.

I can't stress to you enough how your taste buds will change, and your need and love for the taste of sugar will dissipate. It's hard to believe something that you love and crave now may in time taste too sweet, so you'll just need to trust me on this one. I speak from experience having gotten off sugar to the point where I can have it occasionally and it doesn't romance me back into having it all the time. The benefits of living without it are many, and for me include "disappearing" my chronic depression and releasing twenty pounds. It's empowering just to know sugar doesn't have a hold on me anymore!

Another way to enjoy this ice cream alternative is to reverse the proportions of fruit and ice cream and use the ice cream as a topping for fresh fruit. That means you're having mostly fresh fruit with just a little ice cream to dress it up in place of whipped cream for example. It may be hard to think this is a good idea, but once you learn to adjust your eating lifestyle, it will make sense. You'll learn that just a little bit of something can be enough to satisfy a craving.

Additionally, when you're eating really clean and really well, sometimes you can go off the rails and have a piece of cake or a cookie without destroying all the good work you've done. For my birthday recently, we had friends over for dinner and one of them made an amazing cake for me that had zucchini, blueberries, lemon, regular sugar and flour as ingredients. It was delicious, and I enjoyed it immensely; I was also aware I needed to be very good after I had it. I share this so you know I'm not perfect all the time with my eating, and that once you are out of the grip of processed food and sugar, you can have a bit of it once in a while.

I hope however, when you are in this situation, you will remember sugar and processed food are *designed to be addictive*. There is always the danger that one cookie will turn into a box of cookies...or cookies day after day after day...I guess it depends upon your commitment and your resolve not to go back to your old way of eating. It depends upon your determination to eat in a way that supports your long-term health and wellness, both mental and physical. For me, the fear of becoming depressed again is always enough motivation!

Let's revisit our discussion of portion sizes. I know my favorite ice cream stand is now offering a "mini" size as well as a "kiddie" size which may sound tiny, but they're not. It's plenty to satisfy when you really, really want real ice cream. I think this speaks to a general awareness that smaller portions are being demanded now as much as the "all you can eat" phenomenon was popular earlier. This indicates to me there is growing awareness and sensitivity to people wanting and needing to control their portions. It also gives ice cream lovers the chance to enjoy an ice cream treat without ordering what appears to be an entire pint of ice cream stuck on the top of a cone or in a cup.

When you think of changing your eating lifestyle to one that is healthier (notice I didn't say "diet"), I hope you'll be able to envision a slimmer, healthier you who enjoys good whole food. Envision yourself feeling better, having more energy because of your commitment to this change in eating habits, but also envision yourself as someone who can still enjoy an *occasional* treat. It's a process, and it does take commitment; but you can set goals and achieve them with a lifestyle change that supports your health, doesn't leave you starving and still allows you to enjoy life and food!

Again, it's important to remember that sugar and processed foods are designed to be addictive, and there is always the danger that one cookie will turn into a box of cookies or into falling back into the habit of eating cookies day after day. Any serving of these foods, no matter how large or small will generate an inflammatory response in your body. The key is to reduce the level of inflammation so it does not become chronic. In an ideal world, never eating foods that cause any level of inflammation would be most beneficial, but I had to relent on taking this position after one of my coaching clients pushed back and told me, "If I have to eat this way, I won't do it...it's just too hard." I can tell you from personal experience that it becomes easier with time as you begin to feel very differently – very much better in many ways. Feeling so much better is reinforcing and helps you stay on the healthier path of eating a low inflammatory diet.

What about dietary restrictions affecting your ability to eliminate depression with diet?

This is a question I was also asked, and it's an excellent one! When I think of the foods that are best for you to eat, I can't think of a health condition or a dietary restriction that wouldn't embrace eating fresh whole food. If the health condition is diabetes, eating a low inflammatory diet would only support your body. Getting off sugar is critical, and substituting artificial sweeteners is not the answer. Artificial sweeteners have been shown to slow down your metabolism, and if you are prone to depression, again, just a few servings of them can bring on or exacerbate depression!

Your body's ability to heal itself is only aided if you are taking in the proper nutrients. Eating whole food that has not been processed saves your body from having to deal with excess sugar, salt, preservatives and the empty calories that promote inflammation.

The person who asked that question is diabetic, and so I thought this would be a good time to address inflammation and chronic disease as diabetes is one of the many chronic diseases plaguing our population today.

Inflammation and Chronic Disease

We have an amazing amount of control over how we feel, how we age and what chronic diseases we endure. To the extent that every bite of food we take affects our level of inflammation, we are the masters of our own fate health-wise.

We can eat to reduce our body's level of inflammation, or we can choose food that will drastically increase our inflammation which sentences us to struggle with chronic pain and chronic disease.

If you eat a diet largely comprised of foods containing refined sugar, flour, grains, omega-6 oils and trans fats, you are likely living with chronic inflammation. You may say, "I only eat these occasionally", but bear in mind any time you eat food with the refined ingredients listed above, you are creating an inflammatory response in your body. While the response may be low-grade initially, over time it becomes chronic, and that's when we get into real trouble. The good news is that you can reverse the inflammation level in your body.

How you would know if you are living with high inflammation? There is a test you can request your doctor add to your yearly blood work that will measure the level of inflammation in your body. It's called a C-Reactive Protein test, or a CRP test. Just be aware you may have to argue with your doctor to get him or her to include it in your yearly blood work. I know I did.

My primary care doctor insisted I didn't need to have the test, and that my level of inflammation would not be an issue. I *insisted* I wanted the test to verify that. Remember, you have to advocate for yourself within our current allopathic "health care" model. After about five minutes of me insisting, she said, "Fine...I'm not going to argue with you...you can have the test."

She was right; my level of inflammation was not an issue; but I got what I wanted, and now I have a baseline of my body's current level of inflammation. Going forward, I will insist, probably every five years or so, on having another CRP test so I can monitor how I'm doing with managing my own inflammation. This is incredibly important to me as I now believe my chronic depression was caused by inflammation that I had absolutely no idea my eating style was creating. I never had a CRP test during the many years I was depressed, so I have nothing to compare my before and after depression inflammation levels. C-Reactive Protein was discovered back in *1930*, but the connection between CRP and cardiovascular health didn't come to the fore until 1997 so it was not front and center. Recently it has come back into the spotlight and even more so as research shows the link between chronic inflammation (which again the CRP test measures), and many chronic debilitating diseases including depression.

One thing I found curious is that my test results report indicated my CRP value should be less than 5.0 mg/L. I have since read in The DeFlame Diet written in 2016 by Dr. David Seaman, that the CRP value should be less than 1.0 mg/L.

So I pose the question to you...why would allopathic medicine tell us a higher level of inflammation in our bodies is acceptable? This troubles me greatly.

It is very important for you to know what the level of inflammation is in your body as it is a predictor of your predisposition to develop a chronic disease. This could be diabetes, depression, arthritis, cancer, heart disease and so on. In an effort to remain healthy, it is vital to keep the inflammation in your brain and your body as low as possible!

Gut Health

Did you know your gut is now considered to be your second brain? In fact, recent studies show your gut may in part control a great deal of what happens in your brain. While your gut/second brain is not in the driver seat as far as conscious thought or decision making is concerned, about 90% of the fibers in the vagus nerve carry information along that major nerve from your gut to your brain. Among that conveyed information is a status report on the health of your gut. Is it inflamed? If so, that is transmitted to your brain via the vagus nerve.

So how does your gut health impact depression and what can you do to improve the health of your gut? Because your "two brains" are connected and communicating, depression medications meant to improve the state of your mind can unintentionally affect your gut. For example, much of the body's serotonin is located in the bowels. When you are prescribed an SSRI medication (selective serotonin reuptake inhibitor) which is designed to increase serotonin levels, they can upset your GI tract. IBS, or irritable bowel syndrome, occurs when there is too much serotonin in the digestive tract. It's no real mystery that a side effect of these drugs is digestive/intestinal upset as they are meant to increase the serotonin levels.

Irritable bowel syndrome will cause the message to be sent up the vagus nerve that all is not well in the second brain and the digestive system. This message arrives in the brain and is received as verification that "we are inflamed".

I can't impress upon you strongly enough that everything is connected!

My question after sharing this is: Doesn't it make more sense to try to get to the root of the problem with food rather than suppress symptoms with a drug? A drug will cause other problems for which you will be prescribed an additional drug to suppress those symptoms. Think Paxil and its SSRI cousins and Viberzi (a federally controlled substance as it may lead to "dependence"), Linzess (both of these are medications to treat IBS) and their cousins.

Your gut health is also strongly related to the ratio of good bacteria to bad bacteria that exists there. When that is out of balance, it can play an important role in your mental health and your mood. Eating too much sugar and/or fructose... and it's all sugar folks (see page 70 for a refresher on the 60+ names of sugar), causes the release of excess insulin as well as chronic inflammation in your body. *Inflammation negatively affects everything* and is a chief contributor to chronic disease and premature aging. (If you want to stay healthy and slow down your aging process, *get sugar out of your diet*.)

If you suspect an imbalance of bacteria in your gut, and unless you eat an extremely clean, healthy diet, this is probably the case, it would be in your best interest to take a good prebiotic and a good probiotic every day. Personally, I started doing this after a very bad bought of an intestinal bug that just wouldn't quit. I was concerned I was developing IBS which my mother had developed. I could tell within 24 hours of taking the prebiotic and probiotic together that I was improved. Within a few days, my issues had resolved. By the way, many people are familiar with probiotics but not with prebiotics. Prebiotics are insoluble fiber that feeds the probiotic and helps it do its job better and more efficiently. See the Resources section at the end of this book for the prebiotics and probiotics I take every day.

Hunger Hormones and Gut Health

Just as your heart doesn't function independent of your lungs or your brain, so your digestive system, your gut, is connected to everything. In the past few decades, the hunger hormones ghrelin and leptin were discovered.

Ghrelin was discovered in 1999 and is referred to as the "ghrelin gremlin". It is the hormone that makes us feel hungry; it causes our appetite to increase. Ghrelin is produced in the stomach and sends signals to the brain to eat and drink when your stomach is empty. Ok. That works and makes sense.

Leptin was discovered in 1994 and is supposed to say "stop eating...you are full!" Leptin is directly connected with weight and with regulation of our food intake. Leptin is connected to insulin. When you eat, leptin enters the bloodstream and travels to the brain. The more food we consume, the more insulin is produced and the more leptin we make. When we have eaten enough, leptin levels become higher. These higher levels are supposed to signal the brain that we are full, and it's time to stop eating. These higher levels are also supposed to send a signal to the pancreas that you are full and it should stop producing insulin.

This is where it gets tricky, and all the sugar in our diets, both hidden and obvious really harms us. When the insulin the pancreas is pumping out is dealing with too much blood sugar, it stimulates triglyceride production. Triglycerides are a type of fat that exists in the blood, and these triglycerides are stored as fat cells with weight gain being the result. Elevated levels of triglycerides in the blood are indicative of an increased risk of having a stroke. Elevated levels of triglycerides in the bloodstream also interfere with leptin reaching your brain to tell you that you are full, and it's time to stop eating! This is called Leptin Resistance. While the body is releasing leptin as it should, the brain is not correctly responding to the leptin trigger. Very simply, the brain is not getting the message that the stomach is full, so your appetite is not suppressed, and you keep on eating! Your body may be overweight, but your brain thinks you're starving because it doesn't get the message you're full. This is empowering to understand, because it makes so much sense if you're someone who eats and eats and never feels full.

When you have a healthy, correctly functioning gut, your hunger hormone ghrelin correctly tells you when you're hungry, and it's time to eat. Your hunger hormone leptin correctly tells you when you're full; it's time to put down your fork, and push away from the table. When your gut is not healthy, the message that you're full doesn't make it to your brain (again, via the vagus nerve) which is why so many of us can eat and eat and never feel full. It all comes back to your gut and what you're putting in it.

What should you do to have your gut support a life that is not filled with depression and a body that knows when to stop eating? You need to choose foods that support a healthy, upbeat mood; foods that are whole, complex, healthy foods; not foods that are loaded with sugar or that are highly processed carbohydrates which quickly turn to sugar (and then to fat). And you always want to avoid hydrogenated and partially hydrogenated fats that are found in fast food and highly processed food.

Be sure to have some lean protein with every meal, and it's not a good idea to skip meals! Your metabolism can become severely disrupted by skipping meals, and then it goes into a fasting state. Your body thinks you are starving, and it will try to "save you" by storing fat so you don't starve. This makes your metabolism slow down which is not at all what you want to do when you want to improve your mood and quite possibly drop a few pounds!

Elimination of Toxins

When dealing with depression and trying to find answers, it's important to look for causes and not simply go for a medication that suppresses your symptoms. One of the most concerning things for me is that my doctors did not look at what I was eating, nor did they ask me what possible toxins and stressors I was being exposed to in my day to day life.

Did you know that your depression symptoms may be caused or exacerbated by toxins in your world? It's true, and I want to share with you a few of the most common culprits so you can evaluate your exposure to them and perhaps find some relief from your depression symptoms.

Pesticides – Did you know the most common exposure comes from the conventionally grown food we eat? It does! The saying, "You are what you eat" is so true, and it actually goes beyond that to "...and you are what *they eat*". In this case, with conventionally grown food, what *they eat* refers to the pesticides used during the growing process.

Prescription drugs – These sometimes alter our brain chemistry. Some medications like Paxil, for instance, while technically an antidepressant, has a risk of increasing suicidal tendencies. Paxil was my antidepressant of choice, and while I was never suicidal, I was extremely miserable both on and off it. I went on it to try to control my depression and then went off it because I didn't feel well and suffered with a number of side effects, discussed earlier, while taking the drug. You should be absolutely sure to read the fine print on the leaflet you get when you are prescribed a new medication. I advise my clients to keep a daily journal of how you feel so you know when you started taking the meds, and so you know how you feel while taking it. You want to track time, responses and effects. You may think you'll remember, but trust me on this one; you won't.

I know this all sounds like a lot, but I hope you'll stick with me! You will be able to do this in small steps, so I don't want you to feel overwhelmed and toss this book aside. Remember...I've been at this for five years now, so it's a process.

Environmental Pollutants –Next on the hit parade list are environmental pollutants. These include, among others, radon, lead, furnishings in your house that may have been treated with chemicals like formaldehyde, building materials in your home, cleaning products, etc. I am extremely careful, as you should be, to fully read all labels before purchasing any cleaning products. If you see ingredients such as Phthalates (which are found in a lot of household products containing fragrance like air fresheners, dish soap, etc.), perchloroethylene, triclosan, quarternary ammonium compounds, 2-butoxyethanol (which is not required by law to be listed on a label), ammonia, chlorine, and/or sodium hydroxide, it's in your best interest to find a healthier, less toxic alternative. These ingredients are endocrine disruptors, neurotoxins, skin irritants, etc. Additionally, I always look for products that are not animal tested and do not contain ingredients that are animal tested.

Finally, heavy metals found in amalgam fillings, in some fish and in cigarette smoke can influence depression. Mercury is a major culprit in this list, and you should be careful to avoid eating fish that is high in mercury such as tuna and sword fish. Eating *wild caught fish* such as salmon haddock or cod is a better, healthier choice. I suggest avoiding farm raised fish entirely. I don't care how responsibly they tell you it is raised.

Farmed fish are raised in a confined area, and so to keep the fish from becoming sick, they use antibiotics and may also feed them genetically engineered feed. Remembering that *you are what they eat* as well as what you eat, be aware that you are ingesting antibiotics and GMOs by eating farm raised fish.

This is not a complete list of everything in your environment that can affect your mood and can trigger depression, but these are a good place to start evaluating what you are currently exposed to in your daily life.

Please remember not to be overwhelmed or discouraged by the volume of items listed here. This kind of change is a process and a journey. It's one that will benefit you even if you choose to take baby steps toward a final goal of healthier eating and healthier living.

CHAPTER TWELVE

So...What Else Do I Need to Know?

"...epigenetics...allows us to see how environmental factors alter our gene expression...we can literally help control our health and genetic destiny."

~Woodson Merrell

Epige-what?

Epigenetic – The Oxford Dictionary tell us the definition of epigenetic is: "relating to or arising from non-genetic influences on gene expression".

Epigenetics tell the story of why you are truly driving the bus that is your health and your life. The study of epigenetics is fascinating! It's the study of the biological mechanisms that allow you to turn your genes on or off. This is tremendously empowering because in its simplest sense, it gives you the power to "cheat" your gene pool.

How many times have you heard someone say "Cancer runs in my family" or "Everyone in my family is overweight"? Can you imagine being able to beat the odds on your gene pool and not being one of the "everyone"? You can, and epigenetics is the study of how this works. You actually have the ability to turn on or off certain genes, for better or for worse, by controlling what you eat and what you're exposed to in your daily life.

To have a true appreciation for this powerful concept, it's important to understand basic genetics and how those genes we want to influence have control over our bodies. The order of discussion from large to small is this: cells - DNA - genes. We are all made up of cells. In fact, cells are the basic units of every human being, and our cells take their direction from our DNA (deoxyribonucleic acid). Our DNA is comprised of four basic types of bases, A (adenine), C (cytosine), G (guanine) and T (thymine).

It's the order in which these bases occur, or the sequence in which they occur that gives instruction as to who we are and how we are. Are we very private or do we have many friends and share everything? Do we love sweet potatoes and hate how brussel sprouts taste?

Epigenetics controls how our genes are read by our cells. Where we live, what we are exposed to and *how we eat* can turn our genes on or off.

This is very empowering information. Even if depression, diabetes, arthritis, cancer, obesity, etc. "run in your family", it is not in the wood that you will endure them too! What this means is the potential is there to struggle with those chronic conditions, the possibility of those genes turning on is lying in wait there in your gene pool. The control you have is over your diet and your environment. This is so powerful, I have to emphasize again that *what you eat and what you are exposed to* will dictate whether the undesirable genes in your genetic make-up are turned on or not!

Even if you have lived in such a manner that the "undesirable genes" have been turned on, you can turn back the clock by changing your diet and by analyzing and changing what you are exposed to on a daily basis. That's what happened to me. I had turned on my depression genes early in my life. Decades later, quite by accident, I radically changed how I ate, what creams, soaps, shampoos, cleaning products, etc. I used, and I turned my depression genes off.

I know they're still there. In fact I am acutely aware they are still in my gene pool. I respect the power they can have over how I feel and whether I am happy or not. I am careful to eat and live in a manner that keeps those genes in the off position.

You have this power too! The challenge is to be able to choose to eat the right foods, and that doesn't include fast food, doughnuts and soda which are loaded with sugar and bad fats. It can be tough because those foods are highly addictive. In fact, there isn't much that is more highly addictive than sugar. Processed foods are designed to be addictive by the way, and that's a perfect segue into a discussion about sugar...

Sugar!

"Sugar is like a drug. If I have one bite, I need to eat it all. I could eat an entire Panettone in one sitting."

~Sefano Gabbana

What part does sugar play in depression

What part does sugar play in depression? The short answer is a big one! Articles, studies and books including publications by Forbes, U.S. News and books by Dr. Kelly Brogan and Dr. David Perlmutter have documented that sugar consumption, and more especially excess sugar consumption, increases your risk factor for depression and anxiety.

The really challenging part of this problem is that sugar is highly addictive and frankly, sugar does make you feel better even if it's only for a short time. Eating something sweet actually lights up the pleasure centers in your brain before it drops you and leaves you feeling worse than you did before you ate the cake or candy or whatever it was you reached for.

Why does sugar increase our risk of depression? There are several key reasons.

Inflammation! Sugar is a key driver of inflammation in your body and again, inflammation is now known to be a major factor in the development of chronic disease and premature aging. This is in large part due to the fact that sugar makes your system acidic which in turn increases the inflammation level in your body and in your brain.

Switching your diet focus from eating sweet processed foods to eating whole foods and fruit instead of sweets will not only reduce your body's inflammation, it will also help you to drop weight without going on a typical short term diet. If you've been following me for a while, you know I don't believe in dieting. I've never met anyone who has been on a diet long term and/or who has maintained weight loss with a diet long term.

True weight loss and weight maintenance require changing eating habits that will get you to your desired weight goal and keep you there. I realize it's often easier to follow a diet, so I encourage people who do better making life style changes that way to follow a diet like the Mediterranean Diet. That diet is the closest one presently available to the eating habits I adopted that helped me "disappear" my chronic depression. Following a Mediterranean style of eating also helped Rob normalize his blood glucose levels and his cholesterol so he could stop taking the statins that started this whole adventure.

Sugar is also a contributor to leptin resistance. This is huge if you're trying to lose weight! I know I've mentioned these before, but remembering that it's all connected, they deserve more attention during our discussion about sugar and depression. Again, ghrelin and leptin are your "hunger hormones", and their job is to tell you when you are hungry (ghrelin's job) and when you feel full (leptin's assignment). If you eat and eat and don't ever feel full (and that eating includes sugar), you may be suffering with leptin resistance. You won't feel your best if your hormones are out of whack, and you can't stop eating. Scientists are studying the effects of hunger hormones on mood disorders including depression.

What is the Bliss Point of Sugar, and What is its Significance?

"The bliss point is the precise amount of sweetness – no more, no less – that makes food and drink most enjoyable."

~Michael Moss, Salt Sugar Fat

I want to talk about the bliss point of sugar because it highlights in lurid detail just how diabolical the processed food companies are, and just how *their* profit is front and center with no care for *our* health and wellbeing. It follows, that because we are being manipulated to eat so we become unwell, the cascade of woes that include depression are influenced to a great degree by the food choices we make.

Did you know that while it takes an infant several months to develop a taste for salt, we are born with a taste for sugar? Right out of the womb, we want our sweets. That's why the processed food giants enlist the help of scientists to test and determine that perfect amount of sweet that is the "bliss point". If they can nail that dead on, they will sell more cookies, more chips, more bread, more soup and even more peanut butter. Sugar, in some form, is in everything! If you doubt me, check your labels.

The processed food producers taste test with children to see how much sugar they can tolerate before it no longer tastes good to them. The same holds true for adults. We've all eaten something that is just too sweet, and we don't enjoy the flavor. That magical point where it's too good not to eat and then eat some more is what they aim for, and that is called the "bliss point".

It's interesting to note they've also determined once the point of "too sweet" has been achieved we can tolerate food with even more sugar if they just add more salt to the food. We can be pushed beyond our natural "bliss point". Don't like the amount of sweet? We'll just add some more salt and then you'll love it again...

They know that if they design it with enough sugar so it tastes good, we will not be able to resist our cravings for it, and they will sell more of it!

Sugar is pretty hard to top when it comes to creating cravings, and kids can tolerate more sweetness than can adults. Kids crave sweets which are in everything they eat. Foods geared toward kids, such as sugary cereals, you can bet are pushing the envelope on sweetness. *What the processed food companies are doing is teaching our kids what food tastes like or what food should taste like.* They are creating up and coming generations that have learned to eat to become overweight and sick.

The current generations of children are the first expected not to live longer than their parents. The food supply is in large part responsible for this tragedy. In addition, these shorter lived people will suffer with more chronic disease than their parents did and at earlier ages than did their parents. That includes chronic diseases like depression and obesity. Yes, obesity is now a chronic disease!

Did you know 40% of Americans are obese? It's true! It's a shocking and very troubling statistic, and here's the really scary part. The study was done in 2015 and 2016, so it doesn't even give us an idea of what's happening to us now in 2018 and beyond!

The Centers for Disease Control and Prevention report that in our country, 18.5% of children ages 2 to 19 are obese. Children ages 2 to 5 are 13.9% obese; 6 to 11 year olds are 18.4% obese; and 26.9% of young people ages 12 to 19 are obese. There are differences in the rates of obesity racially and ethnically as well with Hispanics and African Americans having higher rates of obesity.

Artificial Sweeteners

If you think you'll dodge the "sugar bullet" by switching to artificial sweeteners, think again. If you're prone to depression, just a couple of servings of an artificial sweetener can trigger a bout of depression. I will not touch them! I try really hard not to preach or wag my teacher finger at people, but I'll make an exception here. Artificial sweeteners are poison! And please believe me when I say it's not in the best interest of your health to drink soda whether it's sweetened with sugar or with artificial sweeteners. The same is true for sweetened sports drinks like Gatorade, health drinks, energy drinks and tea drinks too.

There are so many names of artificial sweeteners, some of which you would never expect to be on the list. Here are a few of them:

- Acesulfame Potassium – marketed as Sunnett and Sweet One
- Aspartame – marketed as Nutrasweet and Equal
- Saccharin – marketed as Sweet 'N Low, Sweet Twin and Sugar Twin
- Sucralose – marketed as Splenda
- Stevia/Rebaudioside – A Sweet Leaf, Sun Crystals, Steviva, Truvia and PureVia

Rather than risk eating artificial sweeteners, if you must, having a little sugar once in a while won't kill you. Please remember though, it's a slippery slope, and a little sugar can become regular sugar which can quickly and easily become an extra five or ten pounds (as well as increase your body's inflammation and trigger diabetes). I speak from experience regarding the extra five or ten pounds. You have to be mindful of what you put in your body, willing to forgive yourself if you get off track and determined to get back on the healthy eating wagon again!

The artificial sweetener aspartame can even cause you to gain weight. While it's marketed as "reduced calorie", "sugar-free" and "diet", it can actually sabotage your efforts to lose weight! The reason for this is that the two main ingredients of aspartame which are phenylalanine and aspartic acid, stimulate the release of insulin and leptin. Insulin and leptin are hormones which instruct your body to store fat. In addition, a significant amount of phenylalanine can drive down your serotonin level, and a low level of serotonin can bring on food cravings.

Artificial sweeteners may sound like a good option... unfortunately, they are not!

What about Soda?

Soda has become an obsession for so many of us. I've left this until the end of the section about sugar and depression and artificial sweeteners and depression, because it comes under both headings.

Whether you drink regular soda or diet soda, you are harming your health in very serious ways. First of all, most regular soda is sweetened with HFC or high fructose corn syrup, so no real sugar in sight. The down side of this goes beyond the issue of a sweetener as much of our corn supply is now GMO (genetically modified) courtesy of Monsanto. The experts are still arguing about the safety or not of GMO food, but for me, anytime you start messing with Mother Nature, you're playing with fire.

What about Gluten and Inflammation?

It is possible gluten contributes to depression in people with non-celiac gluten sensitivity (NCGS). I have learned that I have NCGS, so awareness and avoidance of gluten in my diet I now realize was a key component in my own recovery from depression.

Gluten is what makes bread chewy and "pully". It gives a wonderful texture and mouth feel to foods. Unfortunately, it is this pully, sticky quality that makes gluten difficult to breakdown and digest. Even in people without Celiac Disease and without symptoms of NCGS, gluten can negatively affect parts of the body other than the digestive system. I've heard many people say they don't have a problem with gluten, but it's the unknown affect it has on other organs that is problematic and that makes it a good idea for everyone to manage and reduce their gluten consumption.

When the sticky stuff doesn't breakdown sufficiently and leaves a pasty residue in the gut, your immune system goes on high alert and sends out inflammatory chemicals in an effort to save you. When this high alert goes on unabated, it can damage the wall of the intestines and can leave us with a condition commonly referred to today as "leaky gut" or "leaky gut syndrome".

Gluten is in everything these days including things like creams and shampoos. If you're trying to recover from depression, it's in your best interest to experiment with a gluten free diet for at least a month. You still need to read your labels though! Just because a package says the food is gluten free doesn't mean it's a healthy thing to consume. Gluten free foods can still be loaded with salt, sugar and unhealthy fats so, as always... buyer beware!

You also may want to consider taking a prebiotic and a probiotic every morning. If you do, take them at the same time. I've found many health care professionals suggest a probiotic but not a prebiotic. As I mentioned in Chapter Eleven under the section about Gut Health, adding a prebiotic brought me back from the brink of IBS.

I have good news though! If you're very faithful to a clean diet and you don't have Celiac Disease, once in a while you may be able to tolerate a serving of gluten. I usually save that special treat for pizza. I used to get a gluten free pizza, but then realized gluten free food does not guarantee it is healthy food. I choose carefully when I'm going to fall off the wagon and eat something containing gluten. I wouldn't trade all the gluten in the world for living with depression again however. It's a choice we have to make as individuals. For me, it's just not worth it.

What about Dairy and Inflammation?

Depending upon to whom you listen, dairy can range from ok to good in small amounts to avoid it completely. My take on dairy is that it is best to be avoided. I love cheese and used to love milk and ice cream, so this hasn't been easy for me. It's a decision I've made my peace with though as I do believe dairy is problematic for several reasons.

Dairy is one of the seven foods most likely to cause food allergies. (The other six are sugar and artificial sweeteners, peanuts, gluten, soy, eggs and corn.) Because the odds of an allergic response, which will trigger inflammation in your body and brain are high, dairy is on the "no" list for me, and I suggest it should be for you, too.

Additionally, people who are sensitive to gluten are often sensitive to dairy. I know this is true for me, so if you have Non-Celiac Gluten Sensitivity, which again means you do not have celiac disease but you do have some of its symptoms, chances are you will begin to feel better if you eliminate dairy from your diet.

There are good substitutes now such as almond milk and ice cream made with coconut milk, so you don't have to go without. Just be careful when choosing alternative foods as many times there are sweeteners and oils added that are best avoided.

If you decide to include a small amount of dairy occasionally, what do you need to consider? Dairy products that come from animals organically and/or grass fed, pasture raised are always the best choice. Not even discussing the horrors of factory farming for the animals here, the close quarters in which they are raised makes it necessary to give the animals antibiotics so they don't become sick. Remembering that you are what you eat and you also are what they eat, you are ingesting antibiotics when you consume dairy products from animals who have been medicated this way.

Another issue to consider is the feed factory farmed animals are given. Is it largely corn and soy? If so, the majority of that, courtesy of Monsanto, is now GMO. If you are what *they* eat, you are ingesting GMOs without realizing it. Organic/ non GMO/grass fed is more expensive, but when you know you'll be eating small portions whenever you do eat it, it's a healthier choice!

My advice is to avoid dairy to avoid inflammation and give your body the chance to do what it's designed to do, and that is to heal itself when given the opportunity.

What about Fats?

The Good, the Bad and the Occasional

Contrary to what the no-fat, low-fat craze "fed" us, we need fat in our diets. The kind of fat to eat is the tricky part.

Years ago, we were told to avoid fat at all costs. What we did was to starve our bodies and our brains. We prided ourselves, most of us trying to be healthy did anyway, that we avoided butter, eggs and so on while we used "healthy oils" like canola oil in our cooking, baking, salad dressing, etc. What we were told couldn't have been further from the truth.

Do you ever wonder about the ever increasing numbers of people stricken with Alzheimer's Disease? Our brains are more than sixty percent fat, and our brains suffer when we don't eat healthy fat. The lack of fat is not the only contributing factor to our mental ills now, such as the huge numbers of people suffering with Alzheimer's Disease, dementia and generally declining brain health, but it has had a significant impact.

We learned that not all fat is bad fat! Who knew?? It's the type of fat that is important. The type of fat found in processed foods is the real boogie man in our health as far as fat is concerned.

We need to be sure to include healthy fats in our diets like avocados, nuts and oils like olive, coconut and avocado. Fat is not the enemy. It's the type of fat you eat that will keep you healthy and vital or that will slowly kill you.

The truly bad fats are *trans fats* which are usually labeled as hydrogenated or partially hydrogenated fats. They are artificially produced by adding hydrogen bonds to unsaturated fats. Doing this converts a liquid to a solid *at room temperature.* They do this because the oils they use are cheap (usually canola, soy, sunflower or safflower), and because adding the hydrogen bonds make the oils more stable so they don't spoil as quickly. This guarantees a longer shelf life for the processed food product. The scary part is that there is significant evidence that trans fats contribute to heart disease. While it's a win-win for the food companies, it is deadly for those of us who eat them all the time.

Now for the occasional fat. Saturated fat, demonized for many years by health professionals has come into a more favorable light, but this is with emphasis on "occasional" and in small amounts. Occasional small servings of grass fed beef, if you're a meat eater, are now thought to be less harmful than in past years. The same is true for butter and other saturated fats like cheese. The key is to eat it only occasionally, in small condiment size servings and to source the food carefully. Avoiding factory farmed food products is a good place to start when it comes to choosing food that is better for your health.

CHAPTER THIRTEEN

Addiction and the Processed Food Industry

Is there a link to depression?

"When you go to the grocery store, you find that the cheapest calories are the ones that are going to make you the fattest - the added sugars and fats in processed foods."

~Michael Pollan

How desperate have you ever felt for food? I'm not talking about not eating for a long time. I'm talking about cravings for food you know is not in your best interest to eat. Food like burgers and fries, donuts and pastries, cookies, cake, candy, and the list goes on.

We all have cravings for food, especially when we're eating widely. The really tricky part when you're dealing with depression is that when you're depressed, you want something... anything... that might make you feel better. Maybe it's one cookie or six; maybe it's coffee and donuts out at your favorite corner coffee shop with a friend. The chemistry of what happens when you eat the cookies or the donuts is what's important to understand.

When we eat sugar, we experience a high that's similar to a drug high. In fact, sugar has many times and in many studies been demonstrated to be as addictive, if not more so, than cocaine! Cassie Bjork, R.D., L.D. says, *"Research shows that sugar can be even more addicting than cocaine. Sugar activates the opiate receptors in our brain and affects the reward center, which leads to compulsive behavior, despite the negative consequences like weight gain, headaches, hormone imbalances, and more."*

That same sugar that makes you feel better gives you a bump up in your glucose level, which also makes you feel better. But it doesn't last for long. Your blood sugar drops soon after you experience the high, and that leaves you feeling badly and wanting to feel better by eating more sugar. Your brain can't get a stomach ache, so the inflammation caused by eating the sugar is likely to manifest as depression.

Can you see the treadmill you're on? I was on it too...for decades. But not any longer.

The decision to change is one you alone can make, and I can give you guidance and the benefit of my experience to help you. It doesn't have to be so confusing if you have someone who has gone there before.

What I'm talking about is not a diet. I agree, however, that it's easier for us to think of ways of eating that help us be and feel healthier and help us lose weight as a diet with a specific name. I'll share the path I took with you so you can benefit from the years it's taken me to get to this point with my eating and my mental and physical health.

CHAPTER FOURTEEN

Whole food and how to begin – Take Back Your Kitchen

"Life expectancy would grow by leaps and bounds if green vegetables smelled as good as bacon."

~Doug Larson

Your kitchen has been hijacked by fast food and the processed food companies. Real food is not something many of us often eat either at home or out these days.

Processed food is not really food. It was food before they took all the good out of it, or processed all the good out of it. Then they put back some vitamins and minerals so you don't think it's as bad as it really is, and so they can advertise that it's rich in something. Then they add massive amounts of salt, sugar and fat to make it taste good. When you eat real food, it's the actual food that tastes good. We as a nation eat so poorly, we no longer know the difference. We have been trained by big food to believe processed food tastes like food. It does not.

What is whole food?

By definition, whole food is food which has not been processed. Processed food very often is so lacking in nutrition that the manufacturers add vitamins and nutrients back into that package of Frankenfood. Then they loudly proclaim on the label that it has added whatever it is...vitamin C, fiber, etc. Your body knows the difference between processed food and the real thing. I can speak from experience. I assure you your body will perform much better when your fuel is real, whole food.

There was always a sign that hung in my doctor's office. She has since retired, but she was the closest to a doctor of functional medicine you would ever find in a traditional medical facility. The sign had three lines of print:

- Don't eat anything with more than 5 ingredients
- Don't eat anything your grandmother wouldn't recognize as food
- Don't eat anything that won't eventually rot

Words to live by, and words to stay healthy by too!

Keeping it simple really is in your best interest. Remember, you can't believe the front of the package; that is for marketing, and they don't have to tell the truth there. When you turn over the package and read the ingredients, if they are a mile long, I suggest you put the package of "food" back on the shelf. If you can't pronounce what's in the package, put the package back. If you don't recognize the ingredients, or they just sound like chemicals, put the package back.

I wasn't always this adamant about healthy eating. I was the person who would stop and buy a bag of Cheetos after a bad day at the office and eat the entire bag on the way home. I would hang my hand out of the window of the car to try to lose some of that orange dyed sticky stuff that just wouldn't let go of my fingers. But the taste, the salt, the crunch...it was the best! Until I realized it was part of what was making and keeping me living in the hell that was chronic depression. I had choices, and I made mine. I would never turn back.

Just so you know it wasn't that easy for me, don't forget I was also pretty attached to Peanut M&Ms. I would rationalize that there was protein in them because of the peanuts and that would offset the candy coating and the milk chocolate. I could "disappear" a *large* bag of those in an afternoon. No problem…

I now choose not to eat them any longer either. It's all about choice.

Supplements and Tools to Support a Healthy Mood

I've written that I was on and off antidepressant medications a number of times. I initially expected they would make me feel happy, but I was disappointed when I realized it doesn't work that way. What it does is level you off so you can cope better with your life and with its challenges. Each time I was on the medication, I became dissatisfied with how I felt and opted to get off the medication. Again, I did it with a doctor's supervision as anyone should who decides to stop taking this type of drug.

I ultimately decided to explore alternative means to handle my depression. Here are some of them as well as information on supplements I was not aware may have helped me at the time. Perhaps they will help you. By the way, this is a good time to remind you that I'm not a doctor, and I'm not "prescribing" what you should take. What I am sharing worked for me; please remember to consult your health care professional before taking anything new.

One of the most effective alternatives I've mentioned before was Sam-e. I found it really elevated and stabilized my mood. Sam-e "is a synthetic form of a compound formed naturally in the body from the essential amino acid methionine and adenosine triphosphate (ATP), the energy-producing compound found in all cells in the body". (Cathy Wong, ND). An additional benefit is that it is good for joint health. There were no negative effects from taking this at all for me. It also has anti-aging benefits and has been shown to benefit the brain, liver, joints and other tissues of our bodies. I found it a good one to turn to.

A lack of Vitamin D has been linked to depression. By the way, it can also be linked to osteoarthritis, cancer, heart disease and bone density issues. I discovered this much later in my years of living with depression. While you can get Vitamin D from sun bathing, we now know that the benefits of doing that can be outweighed by the associated risks. Advice on how much D to take as a supplement varies, so consulting a nutritionist on dosage is advisable.

Selenium is next on our list, and has also been shown to have a positive effect on depression. It's an essential trace mineral, and you can get it by eating nuts, beans, seafood and whole grains as well as lean meats if you're a meat eater. Selenium is also good to take to help ward off breast cancer.

Tryptophan plays a big role in the production of serotonin. If "tryptophan" is a new term to you, it is an amino acid. The reason why it's important if you suffer with depression is because serotonin is a neurotransmitter and helps us achieve a feeling of contentment. Foods rich in tryptophan include eggs, spinach, pumpkins, nuts, and peas, so be sure to eat enough of these foods to help your body produce the serotonin it needs for you to feel better.

Omega 3 fatty acids are important to many aspects of a healthy body and a healthy mind. Omega 3s have been shown to improve brain function. To ensure you are getting enough Omega 3s, be sure to eat wild seafood like salmon, sardines and herring. If you are vegetarian or vegan, you can get Omega 3s by eating walnuts, flax seeds, hemp hearts and chia seeds. An added benefit to eating chia seeds is that they help reduce blood pressure!

B vitamins are important as well as they are considered to be anti-stress vitamins. Nutrition experts have found that folic acid (vitamin B9), niacin (vitamin B3), and pyridoxine (vitamin B6) support the amino acid tryptophan to manufacture serotonin, that "feel good" chemical we discussed earlier. Things are so interconnected. It really is very cool!

Finally, I want to mention again a tool I used during the fall and winter months to help my depression. It's a full spectrum light, and I used this tool in conjunction with taking SAMe. My last year as a depressed person was much easier to bear because of these two "tools". You will find a link to a great full spectrum light in the Resources section of this book.

While there is growing evidence suggesting certain foods can improve your mental mood, and I can tell you it was absolutely true for me, using nutrition to fight depression might not work for everyone. If trying to manage depression through nutrition doesn't work, consult a medical professional in order to identify the cause of your depression and the best ways to deal with it.

Organic vs. non-organic

I know organic is more expensive than non-organic products, which is why if you're on a budget, it's important to know when you should definitely go organic.

That's where the list of the Clean Fifteen and the Dirty Dozen from the Environmental Working Group comes in (it's updated every year at EWG.org).

Bottom line for me is that any berry that passes my lips needs to be organic. Apples need to be organic. I can give a little on this if a fruit or vegetable has a hard shell or skin such as an avocado or a banana. I understand we have to work within a budget and deal with the availability of produce. You can make it work for you and eat cleaner without breaking the bank.

Here's the most recent list, courtesy of the Environmental Working Group:

Dirty Dozen

1. Strawberries
2. Spinach
3. Nectarines
4. Apples
5. Grapes
6. Peaches
7. Cherries
8. Pears
9. Tomatoes
10. Celery
11. Potatoes
12. Sweet Bell Peppers

Clean 15

1. Avocados
2. Sweet Corn
3. Pineapples
4. Cabbages
5. Onions
6. Sweet Peas Frozen
7. Papayas
8. Asparagus
9. Mangoes
10. Eggplant
11. Honeydews
12. Kiwis
13. Cantaloupes
14. Cauliflower
15. Broccoli

Copyright © Environmental Working Group, www.ewg.org
Reproduced with permission.

If the package says "organic", is it a safe food choice for me to make?

No! Organic is not always a good choice! That probably sounds crazy, but don't forget about your new commitment to reading labels.

Organic food that is in a box is always processed to some degree. If a food is labeled "organic", it is not necessarily a healthy choice. We see organic jelly beans, potato chips, cookies and all kinds of organic processed foods.

The U.S. Department of Agriculture's National Organic Program has specific guidelines for growing organic foods. The use of synthetic pesticides, fertilizers and growth hormones, antibiotics and genetically modified organisms in their production are restricted. While organic food production offers many bonuses to both people and the environment, it is important to remember *these organic standards have absolutely nothing to do with regulating a food product's nutritional attributes.*

When people were surveyed, the results indicated the perception of a food labeled "organic" was that it was automatically a healthier choice than its non-organic counterpart no matter what the food was.

The fact that the term "organic" appears on so many packages of highly processed foods makes it essential to jump into your label reading mode and find out what is really in that package. This is the only way to determine if it's a good choice. These days, most people just see "organic" and assume it is a healthy choice. You could grow organic poison ivy, but you would still never want to go near it.

For instance, a box of chocolate chip cookies may contain all organic ingredients, but those organic ingredients will still have the same nutritional value as the conventional ones. The flour, sugar, salt, shortening, etc. will not be any more nutritious than the cookie containing the conventional, non-organically grown ingredients. This is a total bummer for everyone, and it really upsets me. I see people buying organic sweets all the time and paying considerably more for them; I'm pretty certain they don't realize it's not a better nutritional choice. Organic sugar does the same damage to your system as conventional sugar does. To your body, sugar is sugar is sugar!

You now know that when you read the back or the side panel, the nutrition facts label tells you about what's inside. That is where you will learn about the calories, what kind and amount of fat is in the product, how much sugar, sodium and so on.

Because the ingredients are listed by weight in descending order, if you see white flour, salt and sweeteners high up on that list, you would be correct to assume you are looking at a highly processed food product regardless of whether it is organic or not.

Some organic products of which you should be wary include sweetened beverages, crackers, candy, energy bars and chips. These are just *organic junk foods* that cost considerably more than their conventional counterparts, are high in calories and don't offer a significant nutrient reward.

Organic sugar is still sugar. I can't say it enough: with all sweeteners, sugar is sugar is sugar. It doesn't matter how healthy or earthy it sounds...agave, organic agave, organic honey, stevia, etc...they are all sugar to your body. The only sweetener that doesn't give you a glucose bump is xylitol, and there are aspects of that of which you need to be mindful.

First, xylitol is extremely toxic to dogs, so if you live with dogs and use xylitol, you must be very very careful they do not eat it. Second, you must be certain the xylitol you choose does not come from China. China is now exporting a cheap imitation of xylitol. The authentic xylitol is made from birch trees.

Organic, non-gmo canola oil is still canola oil, and canola oil is a highly inflammatory oil. Whether it's organic or not, it is not a good choice. It's found in many organic processed foods, and the simple reason they use it is because it's cheap to produce. If the ingredients say, as they often do, sunflower and/or canola oil, you can be pretty certain it will be canola oil. Sunflower oil isn't the greatest choice either while we're on the subject. It is inflammatory as well.

If I'm on the brink of eating something that's not in my health's best interest because I crave a potato chip, and it does still happen to me, I'll get a small bag of organic non-GMO chips that are cooked in olive oil and have sea salt, not regular iodized table salt. There is a brand out there that is relatively easy to find in stores that makes them this way. To be honest, eating potato chips, even ones made like this, is still not your best choice for several reasons. Potatoes have a high glycemic index; they will bump up your glucose levels. They are oily and usually high in salt, and last but not least, no matter how good the ingredients may be, they are still a processed food. But, to admit it, we are all human. Because I want to encourage you to make wise choices when the mood hits you, my hope is that you will seek the treats and cheats that will do you the least harm, that have the least damaging ingredients and that you will commit to having a small portion of them only very occasionally.

Since my recovery from depression, I know that when I get into trouble it is because I become arrogant and overly confident about how good I am feeling, and I assume I no longer need to be so careful about what I eat. That will turn on me if I'm not aware of the slippery slope I am always on, and I don't crank myself back. My wish for you is that you can learn from my mistakes.

CHAPTER FIFTEEN
The Okinawans

"Real food needs no portion control. Your brain knows when it's enough. Only junk food needs portion control."

~Yogesh Verma

It seems most of us would like to lose a few pounds or maybe more than a few. In coaching my clients, I find the easier part is to help them understand how to make better choices in the food they eat. Often, once the changes have been made and the weight loss is still not happening as it should, we need to take a closer look at portion control. Let's discuss portion control and the reasons why it may not be as easy as you might expect.

How do you feel when you've finished eating? Are you full, really full, or do you feel stuffed? Our "All You Can Eat" dining specials don't help us with our weight loss goals. Your body gets used to the feeling of being stuffed.

Earlier we discussed the concept of eating until you're satisfied but not completely full. The people of Okinawa Japan are in one of the very few "blue zones" of the world. Blue zones are areas where people consistently live and are healthy and active to age 100 and beyond. These people practice "hara hachi bu" which means they eat only until they feel about 80% full. Can you eat until you're...let's say... not still hungry, but not yet full and then push away from the table? If you can adopt this habit and practice hara hachi bu, it will go a long way toward helping you achieve your weight loss goals and enjoy healthy, long-term weight management as well as better overall health!

If you want to learn more about the Okinawans' remarkable health and longevity and how it's tied to portion control, I recommend this book written by Dan Buettner, "The Blue Zones, 9 lessons for living longer from the people who've lived the longest". It's a great read!

If you're accustomed to eating until you're very full or even stuffed, how would you go about changing that and putting hara hachi bu into practice? There are a few simple things you can do. One is to use a smaller plate when you eat a meal. We talked about this earlier in the book, and it may sound silly, but a *smaller* meal on a *smaller* plate really does look more appealing than smaller portions lost on a large dinner plate. Just remember there's a lot to be said for visual satisfaction with food.

I did this with the plates I use for my breakfast; I'm not talking about restricting yourself to a small bread plate. Find a few plates that are an in-between bread plate and dinner plate size to get you started to see if this helps you with your portion control.

Another suggestion is to get accustomed to feeling not stuffed, even not completely full. Maybe the best way to put it is to get used to feeling a little bit hungry and being ok with it. I'm not suggesting you should be starving yourself; that's not the way to lose weight, as you'll most likely get so hungry that you'll lose your resolve and will reach for the nearest bag of cookies or chips. Just be aware of how full you feel. Unconscious eating has gotten many of us into a lot of trouble with our weight and with our health.

Just try to remember it's a good practice that when you eat a meal, it's in your best interest to push away from the table before you are completely full and certainly before you are stuffed.

Read about the Okinawans; they've got it right! Be aware of how full you feel and remember to eat mindfully. It's ok to push away from the table and not be stuffed. You will be happier with yourself. You'll drop unwanted pounds, and you will feel and be healthier in the long run.

CHAPTER SIXTEEN

Ok...I Believe You, but What's Left to Eat?

"True healthcare reform starts in your kitchen, not in Washington"

~Anonymous

All this may make a lot of sense to you, but you may be wondering what in the world is left to eat? The answer is... plenty! There is a lot of great food, great easy recipes and food adventures that will delight your palate and help you be healthier and feel better mentally and physically.

If you love food and love to eat, there's a whole new world of food out there waiting to be discovered by you and your taste buds!

Let's talk about breakfast which has become my favorite meal of the day. The basic breakfast for us consists of sliced baby portobello mushrooms lightly sautéed in a little olive oil or avocado oil with a little bit of dried garlic powder and a little organic white pepper. If you don't have issues with high blood pressure, you can use a bit of Pink Himalayan Sea Salt. I grind just a little bit of that on the mushrooms and then put a slice of smoked salmon in the pan. I'm not a fan of the smoked salmon itself as it seems a little too raw to me, so I put it in the pan with the mushrooms and just kind of heated up a little bit on each side; it dries out a bit which I prefer. For a change from the salmon, I'll occasionally have a poached egg or fried egg for my breakfast protein. Add to that a quarter of a ripe avocado (really good, healthy fat for your brain) and a 1/4 - 1/2 cup of fresh berries, and you have a wonderful breakfast that will stay with you for longer than you'd think. This is because there is nothing processed; no simple carbohydrates and sugar to spike your blood glucose and then drop it to make you feel hungry again.

As an aside, we changed our cooking pans as well. No aluminum and no non-stick surfaces. Because of the toxins that are ingested from cooking with aluminum and non-stick, we prefer cast iron or stainless steel cookware.

Lunch can be something small. Hummus with a sliced apple, celery, carrots or cucumbers and a handful of nuts (excluding peanuts, which are not nuts at all and can cause allergies in many people). Sometimes a sliced apple with almond butter is an alternative. You'll be amazed at how "not hungry" you will be during the day.

Dinner should always include some sort of fresh, raw salad. We're not talking about pale lettuce, tomato and cucumber here! We start with a base of organic baby greens like mesclun, arugula, baby kale, & baby spinach. Then we add cucumbers, tomatoes, artichoke hearts, beets, bell pepper, sliced portabello or white mushrooms, berries, figs and fresh cut up fruit, etc. We top the salad with roasted slivered almonds and raw pumpkin seeds (wonderful for the prostate for you guys out there). We'll have that with a small amount of protein. We do eat some fish, so we will have a small serving of wild caught fish or a vegetarian dish like quinoa or wild rice and beans.

Eating Out

Eating out is another challenge. When I'm meeting someone for a meal, my main request when we're choosing a restaurant is..."As long as I can get a good salad, I'm fine." We don't eat out a lot, but when we do, it's a salad and a piece of fish. Honestly though, this means I'm choosing to put myself in the position of knowing I'm almost certainly not eating organic produce. If I choose to put shrimp or salmon on the salad, I will most likely not be eating wild caught seafood. I don't eat out often, but when I do, this is how I have the most control over what I'm eating.

Fish is another entire discussion. Once you look into it you'll discover that farmed fish is not a healthy choice. You should always look for and choose to eat wild caught fish. You also have to be very careful of fish that contain large amounts of mercury like tuna, bluefish and swordfish.

You'll learn to ask for mesclun greens instead of iceberg lettuce which isn't a good food choice because of the pesticides used to grow it. We buy as much as we can find and afford that is organic, and always look for organic mesclun greens, baby spinach, etc.

What do you do for dessert or when you want a treat yourself to something sweet? For the most part you won't crave sweets, and believe it or not, after you stop eating sugar for a while, it will not taste the same if you try it at a later time. I strongly suggest you read <u>Sugar Blues</u> by William Dufty. He wrote the book in 1975, and it was one of the first books to expose the dangers of eating sugar. There are photos of him on the back cover. One taken while he was still eating sugar and the other after he had eliminated it from his diet. The difference is stunning! The information for "Sugar Blues" is included in the reference section of this book.

By the way, if you want to treat yourself and satisfy a craving for something sweet, the easiest thing to do is to have a piece or two of dark chocolate. Choose chocolate that has a cocoa content of 70% or greater, and make it organic if you can find it.

The key to remember is that you want to eat clean whole food that does not cause inflammation in your body. Inflammation is the root cause of disease and aging. There's no pill that will fix it, but the great news is that *you don't need a pill to fix it!* All you need to do is to change the way you eat, and your wonderful body will take care of the rest.

CHAPTER SEVENTEEN

What Happened

"Victory is always possible for the
person who refuses to stop fighting."

~Napoleon Hill

What happened to Rob and to me amazed us both. He started feeling better. His sugar stabilized and normalized; his nerve pain (neuropathy) was greatly reduced. Along with being able to think more clearly, he just had more energy and felt better in general. Keep in mind, this journey we had undertaken was his attempt to come back from being poisoned by years of a very high dose of the statin Lipitor. I was just along for the ride to support his efforts. I do most of the cooking, so I was eating differently too.

What we didn't realize at first was that my depression was disappearing. Have you ever been aware that when something isn't a problem, you don't notice it? You know, your knee is killing you after you bumped it and you notice it all the time until it stops hurting. Then you don't notice it's not hurting anymore. Eventually it occurs to you, but it's not a chronic awareness as it was when the knee was painful.

That's what happened to me! It wasn't until I had to pack up and sell my parents' home where I grew up, which I had been dreading for a very long time, that we knew something about me was dramatically different. At times during the selling process, I was sad and I would get teary, but I wasn't depressed. It's different, and it's hard to explain if you've never experienced chronic depression. The best way I can explain it is that feeling sad can happen during anyone's day and is brought on by an event or a series of thoughts. Feeling depressed is a state of being and it colors your entire world with darkness and despair. Both Rob and I had been dreading the effect the sale of my family home would have on me and what kind of a tailspin of depression it would put me in. But I had no depression, no downward spiral; zero, zip, nada.

This is not to say I wasn't sad at times during the process. It was a sad event and a sad time, but I wasn't depressed...I was appropriately sad. I know the difference, and for those of you who have struggled with depression, you know the difference, too. To be sad at times is normal; to live in a state of abject sadness is not.

There were other things that happened as well. My energy level increased to the point that I was getting up at 5:30 am and getting down to working right away. I was sleeping better. I had a brighter outlook and more optimism than I'd had in a long time; maybe forever in my adult life. People aggravated me less. I was able to roll with the punches better.

I stopped taking things so personally. That improved things at work and at home. I was able to laugh...out loud...and really laugh! In fact, one night this past winter, Rob and I watched Dean Martin Roasts on YouTube until about 2 am. I can't remember laughing that hard or that much.

The capper came when I noticed my clothes were fitting very loosely. I don't weigh myself on a regular basis; I use the way my clothes fit as my every day "scale". I finally got on the scale, and to my surprise, I had dropped 20 lbs! 20 lbs without trying; without dieting at all!!

It wasn't just the 20 lbs either. It was where I lost them. I lost the soft flabby cha-cha on the lady parts that you just can't seem to diet or exercise away. My hips, thighs and butt slimmed down in a way they never had. I still have to make myself go to the gym. Unfortunately, losing 20 lbs doesn't mean you're in great shape, but it does give you hope and less poundage to get into shape.

SECTION Iv

Changing What You Can to Feel Better

Do you surround yourself with people who are uplifting and who challenge you? I don't mean challenge you in an aggressive or mean way, but in a way that propels you onward to be a better version, an ever growing and learning version of the person you are now.

Sometimes self care means making some changes to your surroundings, and sometimes that includes the people around you. Do you have positive people around you, or is there constant drama or anger; constant complaining about people and events? Those emotions don't help you grow; they keep you stuck in a cycle of self pity and smallness. It's not a good place to live.

Recently I had to make a hard decision to remove someone from my life. It was hard, and I didn't feel good about it, but I would have felt worse and it would have been more harmful if I hadn't done it. What I lost was someone I had tried to make work in my life for several years, but who was unbelievably nasty, hateful and angry. I couldn't have that kind of energy around me anymore, so I had to make a hard decision.

Take a look at the people in your life; sometimes change is good.

CHAPTER EIGHTEEN

Take a Look at Your Surroundings

"You just get the vibes of your surroundings and it rubs off on you."

~Gordon Lightfoot

When it comes to living with and combating depression, changing what you can to help you feel better can be really important. While you're figuring out what is causing your depression and taking steps to control or eliminate it, like changing your eating habits and patterns as well as taking a look at personal care and cleaning products for ingredients that may be affecting you, it can be helpful for the short term to change a few simple things that are around you in your world every day.

Surrounding yourself with cheerful objects and furnishings can be uplifting. It may sound silly reading this, but something that makes you smile when you come into a room can go a long way to giving you a boost when you need it. A photo or a painting or even something as small and simple as a pretty feather you may have found that makes you feel good can help. We have a flock of about fifteen turkeys who regularly visit in our yard. I love seeing them because they just do their thing. Sometimes one of them flies up and lands on a fence post where our sheep live. The other day, I went outside, and just off the deck was the most beautiful feather. From the size and color, it was a tail feather from one of the turkeys. It made me smile, and that's a good thing!

What about color? Do you have a favorite color? One that makes you feel uplifted? Think about painting just one wall of a room you spend a good amount of time in that particular favorite color. When you're living with depression, getting things done is often a challenge. The fatigue and hopelessness tends to rob us of our energy, focus and determination required to complete tasks. With this idea of painting a wall, you're not looking at painting an entire room, just one wall. It's a much more doable task. The surprise of coming into the room and seeing that different wall along with the satisfaction of having gotten it done will all be good for you.

Another idea that helped me when I was feeling down was to buy some fresh flowers. It doesn't have to be a huge expensive bouquet. A bouquet of alstroemeria is generally inexpensive, they come in a great variety of colors and they last a long time. Make sure you put them on a table or counter where you can see them and enjoy them! I like to put them on my kitchen table so when I come down the hall in the morning and turn on the light, it shines down over them. It does make me smile!

Do you enjoy candles? The warm light they cast and their different scents can either soothe you or boost your mood. Again, focusing on color, if the candle you're considering comes in different colors, choose a color you really like; one that will enhance your décor and that will brighten your spirits. Go for natural scents that smell good to you. I know I've bought candles that were cheap and that smelled very fake once I lit them...not like anything found in nature, and I couldn't stand the fragrance. It's best to pay a little more and take home a candle with a natural scent you will enjoy.

Speaking of scents, aromatherapy is another tool you may choose to try. Even a simple cup of warm chai tea, with its aromatic properties, can be soothing and can help you feel better, comforted and uplifted. Holding that warm cup on a cold day can be soothing as well. It's funny the little things that can help when you're depressed.

Essential oils are another tool you can put in your arsenal. They can be used with a diffuser, or they can be used in creams on your skin. These are the scents typically used to help combat depression, and they apply to your choice of candles too:

Basil, bergamot, cedarwood, frankincense, geranium, grapefruit, lavender, lemon, jasmine, rose, sandalwood, spruce, orange and ylang ylang.

The citrusy scents tend to stimulate your mood while scents like lavender and jasmine tend to be more calming and relaxing.

Do you have favorite music? Play it and enjoy it both at home and while you're driving in the car. I had a few favorites that I would absolutely blast when I was in the car. I suppose I was trying to drown out my depression and the dark thoughts I was battling. Music can be very uplifting, so don't underestimate its ability to help you feel better! And don't be afraid to dance around the living room if you feel like doing that! Moving is good for you, and is something depressed people don't always do often enough.

I can tell you from experience that dealing with depression is a real life challenge. It can feel like a second job. It's a lot of work to live with depression and still try to function in your daily life. Don't underestimate the benefits of small things that can make you feel a bit better while you sort through and resolve your depression.

CHAPTER NINETEEN

Don't Underestimate the Benefits of Exercise

"If you are in a bad mood, go for a walk. If you are still in a bad mood, go for another walk."

~ Hippocrates

If you've ever struggled with depression and have done any research on it...about what you should be doing to feel better, no doubt you are aware one of the first things you'll hear is that exercise will help you feel better, more upbeat – it will improve your mood. Not what I wanted to hear; just give me a pill to make me feel better, please...

When you're depressed, it's often hard to move never mind get it together to exercise. When some days you don't even want to get out of bed, the prospect of running, going to the gym or just walking around the block can be the last thing you want to consider.

I've never been a very sporty person. I tend to be more naturally sedentary than active. I have to stay on myself to stretch, exercise and keep moving. Exercising causes your body to release endorphins, which trigger positive feelings in your body, as well as the neurotransmitter norepinephrine which is believed to improve our mood. I remember talking with someone who had undergone a heart transplant. He said that he was on the stationary bicycle very shortly after the surgery to try to keep his endorphins surging. He didn't want to give in to the depressive feelings he had about the surgery.

He was a truly remarkable person. I can't be sure I would do the same.

Regular exercise has also been shown to increase self esteem. This is important for people struggling with depression as one of the symptoms is that we often don't feel that great about ourselves. I know I suffered from that, and I was embarrassed and ashamed to admit I was depressed. It was a lot of work to fool the world and to hide my depression. Looking fit and healthy will make anyone feel better!

Exercise increases energy levels. One of the classic symptoms of depression is lack of energy and lack of enthusiasm. Increasing your energy level with regular exercise can only help. This doesn't mean you have to become a gym rat. Go for a walk with a friend, put on some music and dance around by yourself or with others. Run up and down a flight of stairs until you feel it in your legs and you're out of breath. My absolutely must-do exercise every day currently is to run up and down a flight of stairs for ten to fifteen flights. There are easy, instant ways to get some exercise.

Getting your heart rate and your breathing rate up is good for you in so many ways. When you stop and catch your breath, you'll feel considerably more relaxed after expending energy and working off some of your stress and anxiety as well!

So, dance, golf (but forget the golf cart and walk), jog or run, ride your bike; get outside and do some yard work, garden, take a yoga class, a tai chi class or a qi gong class. You have options, and it's fun and exciting to try something new. Maybe your efforts to use exercise to alleviate your depression will lead you to experience a form of exercise you will really enjoy and that will benefit you physically and mentally!

Chapter Twenty

Choose the People Around You Wisely

"Surround yourself with only people
who are going to lift you higher."
~Oprah Winfrey

Sometimes making your life better involves some painful decisions regarding friends and even family.

When you're depressed, you are often not feeling very good about yourself. You can be vulnerable to the opinions and attitudes of others. Here are three suggestions to incorporate into your decisions about the people with whom you surround yourself.

First, you can't choose your family...we all know that. I think most families have some degree of "disfunctionalness" just by virtue of the fact that your family members are there by default; they are not chosen. This means people with diverse personalities and traits are thrown together and expected to get along and thrive. But how do you handle it if your family situation doesn't support you in feeling good about yourself... especially when you're dealing with depression? You need to give yourself permission to take a break if you need one. The world won't end if you skip a gathering. The important thing is to decide if skipping the event will be less traumatic than attending it. If it's something you feel you have to attend, give yourself a time limit for the visit. That way you'll know you're not there feeling badly with no end in sight. This will give you a bit of control which, when you're dealing with depression, can be very helpful.

On to friends. They can be great and can help elevate your mood or they can be toxic. One thing to keep in mind is that as we grow and change, sometimes we outgrow our friends, even previously good friends, and change is necessary. This can be awkward, and admittedly you can find yourself in a situation where you feel badly with a friend and badly because you don't want to be in a friendship with them anymore. Again, it's ok to take a break. Explaining you need to have more time to yourself and that you appreciate the person's understanding can go a long way to taking pressure off you. It can also put some distance between the two of you. Sometimes time just resolves relationships you've outgrown over time if you take a break. People move on...

What about relationships at work? We've all worked with people who complain about everything and everyone, who gossip about others, who spread rumors and who pretty much are poisonous. I've found that people who are negative and gossipy need an audience. If someone like that has latched on to you, take a different attitude, and try not getting involved in the conversations that are negative or unkind about others. When you remove yourself as a willing and engaged audience, you'll most likely find the person will move on to someone else who gives them more feedback and gets involved egging them on. You'll feel better about yourself if you can stay above the office fray and office gossip, too.

Trying these suggestions won't necessarily solve your depression, but they can be useful tools to help you feel better while you're making other lifestyle changes that may help elevate your mood and help alleviate your depression.

SECTION V

Life Now

"Change is the law of life. And those who look only to the past or present are certain to miss the future."

~John F. Kennedy

Life now is very different than the past five decades have been. It would be easy to get lost in regret for the times I've missed while being depressed. It would be easy to mourn the opportunities squandered while feeling badly in general, not having had the energy or the confidence to do things I would love to have done. That's not who I am. At least not anymore.

Life now is more joyful and more directed by me. I feel more positive and more unstoppable than I ever believed possible. I have a ton of energy and optimism, too.

I don't take any antidepressants anymore. My medicine is on my plate every day.

Now I'm able to get up early, get to work writing and creating products that I believe will help others feel and be healthier both mentally and physically. I also still have my real estate practice in place and work at that every day. I still enjoy helping people solve their housing challenges; even after 30+ years! It's like solving a puzzle, and it's never static. The real estate industry, like the health and wellness niche is always changing with new technologies in place to learn and new discoveries being made.

I'm able to laugh and have fun. Something that I couldn't do for most of my life.

CHAPTER TWENTY-ONE
Exercise, Meditation and so on...

"Meditation is the soul's perspective glass."
~Owen Feltham

Meditation – I have read about people who swear meditation "cured" their depression. I use the quotes as one has to be very, very careful about using that four letter word, "cure".

This is so well written by Ocean Malandra that I'm just going to quote this for you:

"When it comes to the real cause of depression, many scientific studies have shown depressed people actually have more <u>asymmetry in their brain function</u> than normal, especially between the right and left frontal lobes; areas responsible for thought and emotional processing. This asymmetry is even considered a marker, or a predictor, of depression in people and is associated with depressive thought patterns like hopelessness.

And what causes this asymmetry? The answer is stress. Depression, like Post Traumatic Stress Disorder (PTSD), is actually <u>caused by brain damage from stress</u>. This explains why numerous aspects of modern life...are linked to depression...

This opens up a can of worms about how society is structured, but it also begs the question: If stress causes depression, can calmness reverse it? <u>Meditation</u>, the age-old technique of focusing on the present in order to dwell in a state of tranquility — the ultimate stress buster.

...a slew of recent studies have found that meditation does actually "shape" the brain; it <u>corrects damage from stress</u>, enhances connectivity between the two lobes and even promotes cell growth in key regions that are underdeveloped in depressed people, like the hippocampus. This means that meditators are changing the actual structure of their brains ..., thereby rewiring their emotional reactions and thought patterns to a calmer baseline on a physical level. This makes them more resilient to depression permanently."

I expect a practice like meditation would help control your mind, your mental state and your emotions, but in my world, the changing of what I ate made all the difference to me. Adjusting my food affected the chemistry of my body and my mind. Different strokes for different folks, I guess.

We do what we call "breathe and pray" at our house, and we practice it before breakfast and dinner. It's not really praying; it's more about taking a few minutes to breathe deeply and then remember the people, events and things in your life for which you are grateful. I'm not traditionally religious, although I was raised to be so. My mother's not very secret dream was that I would marry a minister. That didn't happen... Sorry Mom. I do believe the minute or two this takes twice a day would be a good thing for everyone to do. It slows you down, and the practice of being grateful puts into perspective your day-to-day good stuff and not so good stuff. We'll call them "challenges" for the present.

EFT Tapping – EFT stands for Emotional Freedom Techniques. My first exposure to this was watching the documentary Nick Ortner did, "The Tapping Solution" several years ago. I was struck by the change, by the shift in the people who participated in the program. Not all the participants thrived and showed the same amazing benefit. It really was dependent upon their level of commitment and involvement, as is the case with anything. There was a

Vietnam Veteran who was one of the subjects. I was struck by the reduction in his level of back pain and by his story during the follow up later where he said his children said they had their father back...finally. It was very powerful!

EFT tapping draws on different aspects of alternative medicine including acupuncture, neuro-linguistic programming (NLP), energy medicine, and Thought Field Therapy (TFT).

I admit I have not had the discipline to tap on a regular basis, so I can't give a personal endorsement of the practice. After writing this however, I will be tapping again. Nothing like revisiting something to renew your interest in it!

CHAPTER TWENTY-TWO

How This has Affected My Outlook on the Future

"It is not in the stars to hold our destiny but in ourselves."
~William Shakespeare

Now I have hope. Now I have confidence that when I'm not feeling great, I can look at what I've been eating and make adjustments.

I'm not always perfect at this. I like foods that you like too. They taste good, and they make us feel good for a while. We've talked about how they light up the pleasure centers in our brains.

My new feeling of control is very empowering. I believe that opportunity is there for you to feel it too! We are all a work in progress, and progress and change are most often not linear. I'll give you a recent example.

Recently, I noticed my blood pressure readings were getting higher than they had been historically. They were certainly higher than I wanted them to be. I took a look at what I was eating and doing and made two adjustments; one related to food and one related to activity.

I had never been a lover of salt. I didn't like what was, for me, a kind of metallic taste on my tongue. It turns out that it was the iodized table salt I had always used that I didn't like. Once I discovered Pink Himalayan Salt, it was a different story. Also, I had been using anchovies, both whole and in paste form, in much of my cooking.

As I teach my clients and audiences, when you have a question or concern about food, always turn to the label. So that's what I did. When I realized how much sodium I was eating, as anchovies are very salty, I decided I had to course correct.

I cut way back on my anchovies and Himalayan salt, found a good tasting salt free seasoning to add to my dishes and within a month, my blood pressure had returned to normal.

As an additional aid, if blood pressure is an issue for you, incorporating chia seeds into your meals has been shown to help with lowering blood pressure. You can sprinkle them on salads and add them to smoothies among other uses.

We are all a work in progress. Don't be discouraged ever! Just reassess and make necessary changes. It's important to remember that staying within the framework of eating fresh whole food is a wonderfully healthy way to live. Making adjustments within that framework should be expected from time to time. It's ok; just please don't give up and go back to eating the processed poison.

CHAPTER TWENTY-THREE

It's Rarely a Linear Journey

"Life doesn't get easier or more forgiving,
we get stronger and more resilient."

~Steve Maraboli

This has been a journey of personal discovery and redemption for the most part. A couple of years ago, it was a scary trip to the past. I thought I was getting depressed again. It really frightened me, and I want to share what I wrote at that time to help you know what happened and the process that went along with it:

I haven't felt really depressed in more than two years. As I write this it is fall, and that used to set my depression off badly just by being fall. The flowers die, the light changes, shadows get longer.

I've been told by doctors that my depression triggers were event driven; mostly family deaths. This week, I had two events that triggered those old feelings. I won't bore you with what happened, but the first (and the major event...no pun intended) was family oriented and beyond my control. I got really upset about it, and I was afraid it sent me to the "old depressed place" for a while. To share with you what I was going through, I was "in my head", feeling really down, and not simply sad. It's different. It's a looking inward that's very hard to describe even for me now. I really thought I was depressed again, and *that made me even sadder* and so disappointed. For a few days, it felt as if everything I've been

126

working on, working toward and sharing with you was a lie. The second thing was kind of silly, but on top of the family event, it made me feel even worse.

Full disclosure on this second thing: I love antique cars! Twenty years ago, Rob and I bought a 1960 MGA Roadster, Iris Blue, in very good but very original condition. It needed work, and last year we decided to begin picking away at the restoration process. For you car enthusiasts out there, it's not going to be a "frame-off" restoration, nor will it ever be a "trailer queen". The car was very solid and with very little rust. The transmission needed an overhaul and that means you do the clutch while the "trannie" (transmission) is out of the car. Brakes needed a redo. Dash lights were not completely functioning. The delightful couple from whom we bought the car confessed to us that they were drinking gin and tonics while they were installing a new wiring harness...

We had expected the work to have been done and completed last summer, but it dragged on into the fall. We understood the car was to have been kept indoors, but in the late winter/early spring we drove up to Maine to check on the car as we hadn't been getting good communication from the "expert" working on it. We found it buried in a snow bank in the yard!

There was nothing we could do; unfortunately it was a winter we had much more snow that usual, so we sucked it up and tried to have a frank discussion about work to be done and communication going forward. Have you ever tried to nail Jello to the wall? That's what communicating with our "expert" was like.

The week my family stuff hit, we went north to pick up the car which was finally ready.

What greeted us was less than expected to say the least. The speedometer no longer worked; the temperature gauge didn't work; the convertible top had mildew on the inside from being covered while it sat in the snow bank all winter; the wheel rims had rust on them, and the car generally had bits of rust everywhere from sitting in a snow bank for months. This car had only a couple of very small rust areas when we brought it up north. I was beside myself!! On top of the family stuff, this really did it!

So, now I've shared what I saw and how I felt about what happened. I think it spiraled because *I was afraid I was getting depressed again.*

Once I stopped and realized what was going on, it was clear to me I didn't have to be depressed again. I was ticked off about a family thing and about my car, but aside from being scared I was depressed, it was mostly about how I handled the two things that happened to me.

I now realize I had control over my feelings and that I had the power to choose to relinquish the fear and acknowledge I was just ticked off.

How did I handle it? Well, I was scared enough that I was religious with my diet. No variation, no leeway at all until I came out of this. Diet is what saved me from depression before, and that was the only thing I felt I could turn to.

I'm feeling better now though and am trying to remember what scared me most about how I felt.

There was a feeling of hopelessness about it. A looking inward with no joy and no way out which was how I had lived for many, many years. I lost my ability to reason through the down turn and turn it around. That part scared me. I was just in my head again and feeling hopeless.

It wasn't a good place to live before, and it wasn't a good place to visit again. Even for a few days.

I began to doubt my success with my diet and my victory over depression.

It's been 3 days since I started to feel really badly. I'm feeling better now. Really better, and I'm happy to write that!

Was I depressed, or was I just really hurt by an event? I have to sort this out, but wanted to share it with you anyway. I'm honestly not sure which it was, but it frightened me. I wanted to share even this uncomfortable part of the journey with you that it may give you strength to persevere as well. I drilled down even more strictly on my diet. I stuck with it, and now I can honestly write that I'm feeling better.

Believe me, three days of feeling "depressed" is a lot easier to take than decades of living as a depressed person.

It's all about choice...

"I'd rather wake up to coffee cake..."

I just got an email from a very popular cooking show saying, "Wake up to coffee cake, apple fritters, etc." and I realized... it's all about choice!

I'll be perfectly honest with you. I'd love to wake up to coffee cake and apple fritters, but then I would be depressed, most likely overweight and dealing with a host of oncoming chronic illnesses that would plague me now and in the coming years.

If coffee cake and fritters aren't on the breakfast menu, what is? Delicious food, that's what! I've had a number of clients ask me to come clean about what I actually eat to stay healthy and to lose my chronic depression and unwanted pounds, so I'll be sharing some of my creations with you over the coming weeks and months. I'll do that here, on my blog at http://ThinStrongHealthy.com and on my TV show you can watch on WestfordCat and on my Youtube channel.

Let's talk about breakfast! As our moms told us, it's the most important meal of the day, so here's an idea for a quick delicious breakfast.

I'm a big fan of cooking more than I need for one meal so I can use it again for breakfast or lunch and sometimes again for a dinner creation. This includes roasted veggies in the oven, wild rice and black rice among other foods. Today's breakfast, a quick frittata, included left over wild rice which I cooked last night in vegetable broth and white wine with sea salt, pepper, onion flakes and garlic powder.

Here's how I make it. In a cast iron skillet with some olive oil, add some of the cooked wild rice and heat that up. Then add chopped organic spinach and let that wilt down for a minute; you can use fresh or frozen spinach. (This recipe is for two people and is cooked in a medium sized skillet.) To that, add one organic egg whisked with ¼ cup of unsweetened almond milk and my secret ingredient, a little bit of nutmeg! Nutmeg gives eggs amazing flavor. Turn the heat to low and cover for about 5 minutes.

That's it! You can fold it over or just cut it into wedges. Served with some avocado and cut up fresh fruit, it's a great easy way to enjoy a breakfast that will stay with you.

I showed you exactly how to make it in a video on my latest post at http://thinstronghealthy.com/quick-breakfast-frittata/ so please check it out.

It really is delicious! It will stay with you longer than the coffee cake and fritters and will support your long term health too! Remember it's all about choice, and I want to help you choose to be well!

What to do when you slip back into old eating patterns

When you make significant lifestyle changes, the journey is often not linear. There are bumps, disappointments and setbacks along the way. Here are a few thoughts about what to do when you blow it and slip back into old eating patterns.

If you're most often at home and rarely eat out or with others, it's easier to stay on track. This is not how most of us live however. There are holidays and events, parties, dinners out and vacations where we don't have total control over the food we have available to eat. So what do you do when you slip backwards?

First and foremost, I can tell you from personal experience that drilling down and being very strict with what I'm eating pulls me right back if I've been wandering and eating a little more widely. This is most likely to be a challenge at holiday time or while on vacation. I don't hesitate to have a bite (or two) of dessert at holiday time. That isn't the problem. It's the buildup of the bites that can become the problem. Also, I can become overly confident that I'm doing really well and feeling fine while eating a bit more widely. It can sneak up on me, and before I know it, I begin to feel a little off. Maybe a bit less up, less energetic. I become edgier and less patient as well as just not feeling as positive and upbeat. Sometimes I start to feel down and "in my head" again, which lets me know I need to take a look at how and what I'm eating.

When I haven't been as good as I should have been with my eating, getting back on track is pretty simple. It means lots of green salads with fresh vegetables and a small serving of protein or a vegetarian mixture of rice and beans with nearly every meal. Not only do I feel better in a couple of days, my energy level goes up and frankly, I drop a few pounds.

Be aware of when you feel great and what you're eating and when you don't feel so great and what you're eating. Get a notebook and journal about it. List your food for a few days and how you feel so you can see the cause and results in black and white on the page. This awareness gives you wonderful guidance in your not so linear journey to feeling better mentally and physically through healthy eating!

SECTION VI

This book has been the story of how I accidentally "disappeared" my decades-long battle with chronic depression. I use the word "disappeared", because I am acutely aware my ability to be depressed is still there.

We all have our "stuff", our backgrounds and history that color our lives. We have our gene pool that we now know we can turn on or hold off depending upon how we eat and how we live.

While my own recovery was accidental, I have been very deliberate in trying to solve the mystery of what happened to me. I have never taken for granted that my new found freedom from chronic depression has given me a whole new life.

With this kind of renaissance and renewed health comes great responsibility. I feel a responsibility to those who are still suffering to share my discoveries. To share what I've learned and experienced in an attempt to help others find relief from their own depression.

You don't change your past. It is with you always, and it shapes who you are and how you choose to go forward in your life.

I learned early on to live with sadness, and I want you to know that can be changed. You can learn to live differently, and changing how you eat can be a huge part of that change.

CHAPTER TWENTY-FOUR

How This has Affected My Outlook on the Future

*"Each day holds a surprise. But only
if we expect it can we see, hear, or
feel it when it comes to us..."*

~Henri Nouwen

The edge of sadness – Learning to look at the world with different eyes.

I was always a good student. I was the eldest by default as my older sister had been stillborn. Being the eldest, I wanted to please my parents and they paid great attention to school, homework, activities and achievements. I desperately wanted their approval, and it was hard won. "Don't neglect your studies" was one of my dad's favorite sayings to us. I often joke now that the message I got was "work good, fun bad".

I learned to be self critical; very self critical. A perfectionist in many ways, and to expect criticism as perfection was not often achieved. I was very active in the high school music programs and the musicals. I remember after a performance getting in the car and asking my mother what I could have done better. I don't remember what she said, but I remember she had something to suggest. I remember thinking it would be forthcoming, so I might as well ask for it. I suppose in requesting it, it was perhaps easier to hear and less critical because I had asked for the feedback.

I remember talking to a therapist and telling him about my dad and that he seemed to want to elicit sadness from me at times. My dad had a very tragic early life. He grew up on a farm in Nova Scotia, and they didn't have much. He was the youngest of six kids, and his father died when he was only five years old; his mother died when he was seven. He told me that the day his father died, his father knew it was his time, and so he shook hands with all his children. I find that a sad, formal way to say goodbye to those you love, especially to a five year old child, but that was their way. They were very reserved Protestants, members of the Church of England. When my own dad died, I shook his hand. I was actually holding it, but in my mind and if the others there looked closely, I was shaking it. He was in a coma, but I think he would have liked that I had remembered what he had told me about his father's death.

While I was a child I had no real memory of hugging. Except for my grandfather, and he usually seemed to hug my youngest sister more than my middle sister and me. He even had a special nickname for her. He called her "Toots". I thought that was amazing, and I always wished he had done that with me.

I've always been attracted to and have surrounded myself with Jewish people and with Italians. You can't get much more opposite than that to the stiff upper lip way of my conservative Protestant family life.

To that point, there was no yelling in our house. Except for me and my temper, that is, which my parents and grandmother tried to squash early on. I remember my mother saying that when I was two, I had a temper tantrum while my grandmother was visiting. I was apparently on the ground kicking and screaming and my grandmother poured cold water on me. It seemed everyone was very satisfied that that put an end to those outbursts... except me.

One week about a year ago, I'm not sure what I did. Actually I do suspect I ate a few things that are not on the clean diet list just because I felt like it, and it affected me. I also had a difficult and frustrating week at work and it upset me. These things combined to put me in a bit of a depression. Nothing like what I used to experience, but enough so that it brought it back.

It is useful to remember while I am writing this, but not a pleasant place to go again. I was not as productive as I could have been. It was hard to be out in the world. I was all in my head trying not to feel the way I was feeling and then trying to function normally in spite of how I was feeling. I was very low energy. One thing I did that helped a bit was to laugh; I watched some clips on YouTube of Paul Lynde (who I thought was hysterical on Hollywood Squares) and also some Buddy Hackett appearances on the Tonight Show with Johnny Carson. I also love to watch the comedian, Jim Gaffigan. His bit about Hot Pockets will pull almost anyone out of depression. At least for a while.

In my early life, I learned to look for sadness. I think I learned this from my dad and from some events that happened with him when I was little. He seemed to want me to be sad, and although I tried not to be, I think eventually I learned to look for sadness in everyday occurrences that other people would see happiness and humor in. I once talked about it with a therapist. Oh come on... you don't get your antidepressants unless you talk to one...

His thought was that my father had so much sadness in his early life that he was looking for someone to share it with. I believe he didn't do it to hurt me, but it didn't help me either.

Today, most of the time I look for, see and find the brightness and happiness in things I would have been able to see some sort of sadness in before. Early on in my "recovery", if I started to see the sadness, I would get concerned, and frankly, a little afraid, that I was going to become depressed again. I spent so much of my life battling a dark mood most days.

Now, nearly five years later, I can say with confidence this new way of eating whole, nourishing food has changed my life. I feel better physically, mentally and emotionally. I love not being depressed. Do I still get nervous sometimes if I have an "off day"? You bet I do! The memories and the suffering caused by decades of depression are not forgotten in a few months or even a few years. Maybe it will never be forgotten.

The more time that goes by however, the more confident I am that this is not a passing phase. I have control over my mental state based on the low inflammatory diet I choose to eat. I now know it's not a short term feel-good phase I'm going through for some unknown reason. The years I've been eating this way is the time I've been living without depression as I once knew it.

I am in general more confident, more relaxed, more optimistic and more excited about the future than I remember being, perhaps ever.

Chapter Twenty Five
Preventing a Backslide

"Every day is not perfect."

~Brett Favre

I admit that once in a while I fall off the wagon. The eating healthy food wagon that is.

One year, I decided to bake a cake that was a recipe handed down from my Grandmother. I decided to break out the white flour and sugar. The cake looked incredible, smelled chocolaty and Rob was horrified when I informed him I fully intended to have a piece.

As I've said, I'm not perfect...

The cake was really good, but it was funny because it didn't taste as good I remembered it tasting. I had changed a few things. The fat free sour cream was now fully fatted, the promise light was now real butter, and the egg whites or egg beaters were real whole eggs. I'm not sure if these changes or the changes in my taste buds were the difference, but it still tasted pretty good, and I had a good sized piece of it.

I wish I could convey to those of you who are still eating widely and still struggling with depression and anxiety what a difference changing how you eat can make in your life. All I wish to do is share my personal experiences, challenges and victories and hope it helps you find your path to better health and a happier you!

Changing how you eat is a journey, and the destination is optimal health. The important part is to begin.

Don't think I'm a natural at this stuff. I loved my pizza, my Panini sandwiches and my ice cream! Will I ever eat outside my "new box"? Yes, but just a small occasional taste. At the holidays, I have enjoyed small servings of desserts I hadn't had in a very long time. They tasted good, and I enjoyed them. But honestly, they didn't taste as good as I remembered them tasting. They certainly didn't taste "risking depression" good!

I love the way I eat now. Admittedly it's sometimes a bit awkward. For instance at work, they have lunch meetings which include pizza and salad or sometimes sandwiches, chips, *huge* chocolate chip cookies and soda. I explain why I'm not eating the food, and either people get it or they don't. That's their choice, but I'm doing what is best and right for me.

One of my coaching clients has confided in me that she keeps trying to change how she eats. She'll get started on a diet or a new fad way of eating and will do really well. Then she'll go completely off the rails for a day or two whether it's at holiday time or while on vacation or just going out with friends. She gets disgusted with herself and completely gives up trying.

> *"Look for Progress Not Perfection!*
> *If you screw up one day, don't give up!*
> *Forgive yourself and begin again.*
> *Screwing up does not equal failure.*
> *Giving up does."*
>
> ~ Cheryl A Major

The biggest thing that prevents a back slide for me, is frankly, **fear**! Fear that comes from the fact that for all the time I've been eating this way, I've felt so good, so level in my mood, so free from worrying about depression and the debilitating effect it had on my world. I don't ever want to go back to how I felt for all those years. It's not worth a few minutes of pleasure eating food I know isn't good for me anyway.

Fast forward a year later, and as I'm editing and continuing to write this book, I have to add another paragraph about what prevents a back slide for me. A year ago, it was fear. Today, I choose to eat this way. I don't do it out of fear...well, maybe I partly choose out of fear, but mostly, I choose to feel good, to be well, to live a happy life and to be a person who enjoys a balanced mood most of the time. I say most of the time because as we know, life happens.

It is my sincere hope that this gives *you* hope that you can rescue yourself from depression. And, just think, you may lose a few pounds along the way.

Summary/Conclusion

I want to share with you what I wrote after having been on my revised eating plan for more than a year...

I'm now approaching my second fall eating this way. I feel so different. I used to despise fall, and the mere mention of it would fill me with dread. In the middle of this past summer (it's August as I write this), someone mentioned the coming fall in passing, and what occurred to me was that the leaves would be beautiful and the air would be cool. It would be different from summer and that would be good. Don't misunderstand me, summer is still my favorite season. I love the heat. Even the humidity is ok with me, but to be ok with fall was a remarkable event for me.

I can't tell you how strange it is when I observe myself thinking these thoughts. It's reinforcing and it's liberating!

Last year, when I wrote that I was doing well during the autumn months, I was honestly still scared of fall and of how I might feel. I had been feeling so good and was so changed from the decades-long life as my struggling depressed self, that the oncoming fall was an experiment for me. As it approached, I was wary. How would I feel? Had I just been going through a good period for some unexplained reason? I still didn't have confidence in my new found level mood. I was still waiting for the axe to drop.

The more time that passes, and frankly, the more falls I experience without depression and dread, the more confidence I have that I have relieved myself of decades of depression. Helped myself without drugs or therapies. Just by changing how I eat.

That was then. This is now; it's 2018:

I'm planning to go more or less off my healthy diet, and here's why.

Rob and I have a trip planned to Portugal for late summer, 2018. Our last trip to Europe was to Italy back in 1996. We were supposed to go back to France in 2001, but we were scheduled to fly out of Boston on the evening of September 11th, 2001. Needless to say, we did not go.

As everyone who knows me is aware, I eat carefully. Part of the reason is to stay healthy, and part of the reason is that eating the way I do "disappeared" what for me was a battle with chronic depression. When I hit Portugal, however, that plan is going off the rails for however long I'm there. I won't go totally crazy though. My goal will be to "Eat Your Blues Away" in Portugal!

What I'm curious about is the possibility that this going off the rails plan will bring on depression again. I know my mood well, and I'll be able to tell if it's getting weird with my head and my mood. If it does, I'll switch back to the straight and narrow. But hey, a girl's gotta go nuts once in a while!!

I'm also curious to see if eating the food in Portugal, which I know is vastly different quality-wise from the food we get here, affects me differently. For instance, wheat in the United States has been hybridized to be shorter, faster growing and most definitely to be higher in gluten. Gluten is highly addictive (they spray it on your McFries to keep you coming back for more).

In addition, Europeans haven't had the GMO food inflicted upon them as we have here. It's easier to eat widely and safely as the Europeans embrace good food. I guess you can say it's what their culture is built on.

What about sweets and desserts! Well, I plan to sample those in moderation. I don't find sugar tastes like it used to when I do eat it. It almost tastes kind of bitter, if that makes any sense. I don't love the sweetness like I used to. I've been on this diet and mostly sugar free for over five years now. I've read that Portugal is known for its chocolate mousse, so I will definitely want to try that!

I'm really looking forward to another adventure in Europe and to loving their food again. Until I get off that plane though, I'll be on the straight and narrow and "in training" for my vacation in Portugal!

And another thing...what about your children?

Did you know Japanese children are projected to live the longest, healthiest, leanest lives of all children in the world? It's true, and Japanese parents know the importance of teaching their children about food.

When we live in a country with abundant food, why are we always struggling with the ever increasing epidemics of childhood obesity and childhood diabetes? It's because of the food we eat! But, if it were a simple thing to change and just start eating healthy meals and snacks, we would have done it by now.

The fact is that our food supply, our SAD diet (Standard American diet) is killing all of us. It's sentencing our children to lives of dealing with chronic disease at an earlier age and a shorter life span than we are projected to enjoy. Why is it so hard to stop eating our favorite processed foods and snacks, and what can we do to change that?

The answer is simple, and it's complicated at the same time. Simple because or processed foods, loaded with bad fats and sugars, and our huge "all you can eat" portions are killing us. Complicated because those same processed foods are designed by the processed food companies to be addictive.

Have you ever heard of an addict just deciding one day to stop shooting up heroin or snorting cocaine? It's not that simple! I've written earlier about how processed foods affect our brains the same way those drugs affect them. It's just not that simple. If you understand how to begin to change though, and you're willing to take measured consistent steps toward healthy eating, you have a real chance for you and your children to enjoy healthier, happier lives. But it takes knowledge and commitment.

CHILDREN AND OBESITY

Here are some suggestions and ideas to help you and your children get started on a different path toward a healthy future by making smart food choices rather than toward possible chronic disease and a shorter lifespan.

Explore new foods. It's fun to have a different country-themed meal once in a while. Mediterranean is typically healthy, so having an Italian meal is a good way to start. That doesn't mean a huge plate of pasta and unlimited bread though. Italians eat lots of fresh fruits and vegetables along with lean protein.

Another night, enjoy a Japanese meal. This would include fish or lean protein like chicken with brown or black rice and fresh or lightly steamed or stir-fried vegetables.

Have a new rule. If you have a picky eater in the house, he or she has to take at least one bite of something new before they are excused from the table. (It's a good idea, by the way, to eat a meal around the table rather than in front of the TV or on the go.) This one bite rule was the rule in my house growing up. I know I like food today I would otherwise have refused to try.

Change the size of your plates. Here is the suggestion I've made at least a couple of times already. It's another lesson borrowed from the Japanese. They serve food on smaller plates. Follow their good example and make those huge dinner plates disappear! Portion control is so important for weight loss, healthy weight maintenance and for you and your children's overall long term health

Make eating an adventure. Get the kids involved with making meals! I know we're all busy, but take a little time to prepare a meal with your children and a few minutes to enjoy at least one meal together each day.

Set a good example. If you enjoy the healthy foods and snacks you want your children to eat, and you show your children you enjoy eating them, you will be a good role model for your kids. The odds are you will lose weight and will live a leaner, healthier life too!

We should all take a lesson from the Japanese with their healthy children and should teach our children about good food. We need to teach our children what real food should taste like. If they've been eating the Standard American Diet, they think food should taste like processed chicken tenders and pop tarts.

Addendum

Taking an antidepressant? If so, you're one of the many who are!

Did you know that more than 30 million people in this country, that's one in seven women and 20% of women over the age of forty, take some form of an antidepressant.

We are told depression is caused by a chemical imbalance in the brain; that we depressed people have reduced amounts of neurotransmitters such as serotonin and norepinephrine in our brains. But what if that is not always the case? What if the root cause of our depression is often something we have complete control over? *What if it is in fact caused by inflammation in our bodies and our brains that has been triggered by our diet, our environment and our sedentary lifestyle?*

If the answer to the preceding question is "yes, it is caused by inflammation", I sense two outcomes. First, we have tremendous power over how we feel mentally and physically, which is exciting and tremendously empowering; and second, we have to let go of our expectation that taking a pill and changing nothing else will "fix" us.

Remember that antidepressants have side effects some of which include weight gain, liver damage, suicidal or homicidal behavior and reduced cognitive function. I shared earlier that cognitive disfunction was something I experienced when I took antidepressants. They made my head feel like Jello, and I had trouble assimilating information and thinking clearly.

What doctors don't often tell you when you start taking these drugs, is that they are extremely difficult to stop taking. Called "discontinuation syndrome" in the medical field, you must wean yourself off them with a doctor's guidance or you can get yourself into a lot of trouble. I know someone who has taken antidepressants for decades. Trying to stop causes extreme anxiety attacks, and as hard as she has tried, she has not been able to wean herself off them.

So this begs the question: *Where is your power to feel better?* Where does your power lie and how can you tap into your power? The answer is both simple and difficult. I say that not to be obtuse, but because the simplicity lies, in great part, in what you eat, what you expose yourself to in your environment, and whether you are sufficiently physically active or sedentary. The difficulty lies in our Standard American Diet, our chemical laden creams, shampoos, cosmetics and cleaning products and our choice to sit on the couch and watch TV or play video games rather than go outside and putter in the garden or go for a walk.

You can begin very simply by making some small changes. At the very least, begin by reducing or eliminating sugar, dairy and gluten. It's critical to rescue your poor ailing gut, now designated as your "second brain", by taking a good prebiotic and probiotic every morning. Our American diet has left our gut flora in a terrible state giving us leaky gut, which amps up the inflammation in our bodies and our brains. This contributes to food cravings, obesity, depression and so much else that challenges our health.

Perhaps easiest of all is to make an effort to eat mindfully. That's not changing what you are eating. You are just becoming aware of what you're eating. I challenge you to become aware of what's being touted to you as a "good meal". When you watch food advertised on TV, notice if that fast food meal has anything green or colorful on the plate, or is it just beige soft stuff? Look at your own plate of food at your next meal with those same critical eyes.

Awareness is your first step to making positive changes and to feeling better both mentally and physically. I rescued myself from decades of living with depression by making significant changes. You can do it too, and you will be more successful if you commit to changes in lifestyle to put your body back in balance.

Treat your body well, and it will reward you. Now, get up and go for a walk!

Resources

Clean Fifteen and the Dirty Dozen – Environmental Working Group http://EWG.org

Prebiotics: Klaire Labs Biotagen Prebiotic

Probiotics: Jarrow Formula Probiotic

Blood Pressure Cuff: Omron Portable Blood Pressure Tracker

SAMe: Jarrow Formulas SAM-e

Full Spectrum Light: Verilux Compact Portable Light

Books:

Salt Sugar Fat by Michael Moss

Sugar Blues by William Dufty

The Blood Sugar Solution by Dr. Mark Hyman

The DeFlame Diet by Dr. David Seaman

The Blue Zones by Dan Buettner

About the Author

Cheryl A Major has been on a healthy eating journey for many years. Starting at age 28 when she discovered she was severely hypoglycemic, she's adjusted and changed her diet and has influenced the eating habits of those around her.

In the past few years, this journey has led her to remove all processed foods, gluten and preservatives from her diet. The change in how she feels both physically and emotionally has been the inspiration for her blog, http://ThinStrongHealthy.com, her TV show by the same name and for this book. Changing her diet "disappeared" the chronic depression that had been a struggle since she was a teenager; an unexpected result of these food changes was a significant drop in weight!

Imagine Americans changing the way they eat, feeling better and losing weight. And doing this without subjecting themselves to "diets" and the resulting yo-yo lose-then-gain pattern we see happen all the time. It can be a reality!

Cheryl's mission is to share her discoveries to benefit those around her whether it's in West Suburban Boston where she lives or with her nation-wide internet community!

Cheryl says, "I didn't learn this... I live it!"

Made in the USA
Middletown, DE
15 January 2020